A journey of a Commertial Artist to Entrepreneur

VINOD PATIL

3Dpreneur

Building my business of 3D Visualisation multi-dimensionally

Qurate
quratebooks.com
Because everyone has a story to tell

This book is created by:

BookMark

A Division of:

R&S Enterprises

It's time to tell your story

https://rsprintingsolutions.com/book-creation-services/

3D Preneur
Vinod Patil

Published by Qurate Books Pvt Ltd.

First Published in 2022

ISBN: 978-93-94600-28-7

Printed in India

Qurate
quratebooks.com
Because everyone has a story to tell

Qurate Books Pvt. Ltd.
Goa 403523, India
www.quratebooks.com
Tel: 1800-210-6527, **Email:** info@quratebooks.com

Foreword

I've known Vinod for over a decade since we worked together at an advertising agency. There was an air of genuinity to him, and the spark of creativity shone brightly even at that time. His grasp of the world around him was uncanny, and unlike most creative, he looked to go deeper. His thirst for knowledge is insatiable, and the need to excel equally so.

I moved on from the agency to pursue my calling of coaching and training. We parted ways from the agency much later. However, we remained in touch.

My coaching process was different since I married the science of numerology with a workable coaching approach to inspire transformation and change. One day, he called to share that he was at crossroads and needed some direction to pursue his calling – should he continue being in a job or venture out on his own. Needless to say, with his never-say-die spirit and need to evolve, a solo was the way to go. He was quick on the uptake, and our sessions were immersive.

While he was a friend and remained one, objectivity remained prime. I saw him morph into an entrepreneur working in an area unbeknownst to him – 3D visualising, with sharper business acumen and superior talent. When we met again next, he had evolved. He's a fighter, a determined person, a great student, a good listener, an early adapter, hungry to learn and, importantly, grounded.

In the past few years, his knowledge through the expanse of work he has taken on has enriched him, and this book is a way to give back and share the knowledge with those who needn't struggle to understand the business. I'm proud of Vinod, and I've seen it all - his trials and victory!

There are innumerable takeaways – like how to scale, how to professionalise a business predominantly known to be of freelancers, how to adapt to management techniques we only learn but don't implement like being asset light, nimble in operations, outsource, stick to your core, push the boundaries etc. etc.

The very first chapter talks about the price equation. It is tough to explain "how he charges", but without any fear, the gutsy Vinod I know has presented where he is coming from without any insecurity. His clients would be happy to read how he values his business and his work without compromising anywhere. This is a real eye-opener many competitors would appreciate as these lift the industry standards.

Farzana Suri

Victory Coach

Numerologist | Trainer | Speaker

Preface

The business of 3D visualization I run does appear relatively easy than it is. It all depends on how you model your company; I've done it as an entrepreneur from day one. I want the reader to note the keyword used in my last line. It is a "business," and I call myself an entrepreneur and not someone who is a solopreneur or freelancer.

I want people, particularly aspiring entrepreneurs, not to get bogged down by any challenges when they start their business. There are no barriers unless you allow them to come to you. All you need is the right mindset.

"3Dpreneur" is how I see it, and I want many to be inspired by it. Unless you don't position yourself rightly, the world will never do that for you. The term "preneur" means a person who takes (something), especially one who accepts an offer or takes a bet. In my brief career, I've accepted bets for sure. Bet to succeed, perform against all odds, which repeatedly gives a new dimension to my 3D visualization business.

The three-strong dimensions of my business are hunger to succeed, perform against all odds, and deliver consistently.

This book expresses my business, which I am incredibly passionate about. The objective was to perform with creative freedom. As an entrepreneur, not loving the art of making money is not right, but that's not the only objective.

I want the reader to understand, absorb and gauge how seriously and professionally we take our business of 3D visualization.

Entrepreneurship gets you freedom. It gives you the freedom to perform in your way, take risks, take responsibilities, try unconventional ways, and multitask. Still, these are all your decisions at the end of the day. You do not have anyone on your top whom you are answerable, but you must look into the mirror and repeatedly ask whether you are doing right. I was happily working in the advertising sector. I earned a good salary in 2015 when the entrepreneurial bug bit me. But what happened? Why did I take this path? There were people all around me discouraging me from quitting my job but urging me to work hard to excel further. My friends joked about me and would wonder what was wrong with my thinking. I would avoid meeting them, would ignore their messages, and was also shy about telling about myself. I would skip social gatherings also.

The freedom I mentioned earlier was also to make sure I don't get into a rat race, or get so busy working for someone else that I lose my quality of life. I told myself I didn't want to fall into the same trap; I needed to change these working patterns, clients' expectations, and industry standards in whichever way. I'm not saying to change the world. I just wanted to see change in me and my company. I started following some ethics, processes, and setting systems to professionalize my business as much as possible. Not compromising on quality, service, no negligence at the same, not compromising on costs on unhealthy lifestyles of my team members or encouraging late working hours.

Family life matters to me the most, and I want my team to experience the same. I want to see happy faces coming to the office.

My family was pretty supportive, but out of their concern would always tell me to go back to employment and take up a stable job. Coming from a conservative middle-class Maharashtrian family, this was expected. Still, I wanted to prove a point that I could succeed in business. It was a tough time but what got me going was nothing but my passion. I genuinely believe that if I can set myself well, learn the industry's tricks, and further add value and improvise, there's good scope here. I was conscious of the fact that my industry was not considered professional. Freelancers and small teams deliver inconsistently, and they have commoditized the market. So how would I change this?

I'm an optimist, and though just a Diploma holder, I am confident about my game and strengths. I knew the right mindset would take me places. There was never any restriction in my mind regarding how one will succeed. With good support from my family and subsequently from my wife, a Degree holder from J.J School of Arts, our combination and teamwork have helped us further scale up our business.

Motivation is another keyword in my life. I wanted to

stay motivated during the challenging peak Covid times of lockdowns. I am inspired by the well-known actor and motivational speaker Ashish Vidyarthi whom I follow. He once said, “a motivational speaker is one because he needs to be motivated.” I chose to educate youngsters during these times and conducted online training on “How to start and build a 3D rendering and animation business”. Around 400 people I could talk to in those months, and that gave me tremendous satisfaction. They inspired me, the questions they asked, and the mentoring I could do. The idea was to groom, educate and motivate the participants on 3D renderings and animation.

My motivation rubs on my team today. Today, the team members all know we have a larger purpose of chasing and achieving. Our horizons are widening only because of this approach, which is delivered in the work we do for our clients. We’ve always set high benchmarks in performance and delivery.

Another strong reason I wanted to write this book is that I want people to know the actual value of our business. We are experts and possess a sense of authority and tremendous credibility – all earned from all these years of experience and consistency.

Today, as we grow exponentially, we have plans to scale our business further and add value that no one else in our industry can think of. We are a young team full of energy, grit, and determination, always wanting to excel in our chosen field and delight our customers.

I want the reader to change their perception of the 3D visualization field, and we will do every bit to contribute.

Feel free to write to me further at vinod@weaverbird.co.in

Vinod Patil

About Me

"Winners never quit, and quitters never win."

Vince Lombardi

Nothing couldn't have been so apt for me as an inspirational sentence than the above.

In my brief career, I've seen it all and experienced the excitement, joy, failure, depression to success that very few can experience in their lifetime.

What would be the top traits of an entrepreneurial mindset in the initial stages?

- Risk-taker
- Stubbornness

- Unplanned
- Going by instincts
- Ignoring the finances
- Considering only sales as a success
- Lack of vendor management skills
- Short-tempered

I was everything mentioned above, and I repeatedly suffered because of this.

Let me start with my childhood. Born in a sleepy town near Dhule, my father was already in Mumbai, working in a renowned company. We used to stay in a small room along with my elder brother. We are from the farmer community, and my grandfather (mother's father) carried a lot of goodwill in the village. My father's family was not financially sound. We used to get the farm products from our village regularly. My grandfather also supported us financially in the early years when we used to stay in Mulund, Mumbai. The place we used to stay had a lot of mixed communities. We used to stay with people from various backgrounds, namely, Gujaratis, Punjabis, North Indians, and even Sindhis. This communal mix helped me learn about diverse cultures and live in cosmopolitan surroundings.

I didn't live a glorified life then, and my father, a hardworking, educated M.A Special in those days, used to struggle to meet both ends. He always wanted us to study and get a good job for ourselves. We are three brothers, and I'm the one in the middle. I used to get hammered from both sides.

I was never interested in studies, but my school H. K. Gidwani School, is the one that laid my foundation. Art, drawing, and creative building were something I liked always. This liking was noticed by none other than my school teacher Ms. Anupama when I was in sixth grade, who spoke to my parents about it. She almost became my parent at school, always encouraging my creativity and drawing skills. My parents, mainly my father, were not in sync with this and wanted me to study, but who could help? I was an average student. I don't blame his thinking also because such professions were at their nascent stage then, and people couldn't imagine making big money.

Had Anupama teacher not told me to be patient and take my studies seriously, I wouldn't have passed the standard tenth also. She urged me to pass the SSC examination to get admission for my Diploma studies later. She urged me to appear for the elementary exams in drawing, which gave me a lot of confidence. I knew I was good at drawing.

One of my father's friends eventually noticed this art of mine. He suggested to him that I needed to study at the Sir J. J School of Art, but I went to L.S. Raheja School of Art in Bandra (Formerly known as Bandra School of Art). Traveling to Bandra for someone who had hardly moved outside Mulund was a big task. My father also gave me a mobile phone to ensure I was in touch with them regularly. Slowly my father started to understand I was made for the creative line, and his support only increased with each passing day.

My first step toward success was when I got selected for an internship out of forty students in my college. I was delighted, and my parents were equally thrilled as it was a paid internship of rupees two thousand per month. My journey had begun.

I worked for three companies before I started my venture in 3D visualization. Beyond Design, Art Advertising, and Red Communication, were the three companies where I learned everything.

I remember I was lucky the day when Mumbai was under the terrorist attacks. I left office early that day and missed the episode narrowly at the VT station then. The whole family was concerned as everyone knew I used to work in Nariman Point and used to come to the VT station to catch a train back home for Mulund in the evenings.

****

My first step toward success was when I was selected for an internship out of forty students in my college. I was delighted, and my parents were equally thrilled as it was a paid internship of rupees two thousand per month. My journey had begun.

****

My profile was of a commercial artist in all the places I worked. I had passed the Diploma in Commercial Art, and the jobs coming my way were always for this function. My jobs got me good exposure to the glamour world also. We used to shoot for advertising films, and I got opportunities to work on brands such as Macro Man, which had Hrithik Roshan as the model. I used to go to shoots early mornings at Juhu beach and started enjoying all this. I started enjoying glamour, fame, and people talking about my work profile and praising me for my achievement. It was here I met my good friend and mentor at Red Design, with whom I always stayed connected. His name is Abhay Lutade. My association goes back with him since the year 2009.

Life was running well around all this, and then came a turning point. I knew somewhere I was made for business and not for working for someone else all my life.

I took a small loan from my father from his provident fund to start a T-shirt designing and selling venture under a brand called Y-Rus. I used to create designs, found a few suppliers, and started selling these door-to-door on my bike in shops and boutiques in areas such as Bandra, Mulund, etc. I never used to get paid for these as the unsold stock was returned to me, but my suppliers started chasing me for money. The financial burden started mounting, and I lost sleep over all this. I didn't tell all this to my father, who thought I was working very hard, running everywhere and supplying T-Shirts to a good number of stores. But my story was different. The desperation reached its peak, and the losses were only mounting. I started borrowing money from others to pay people. I used to cry sitting alone on my terrace. I realized then the importance of why my father used to tell me to study and get a good livelihood for myself. All this hit me badly, and I was on the verge of collapse. A complete mental disaster was staring at me to the extent of even suicidal thoughts.

Finally, I told my father about all this, and the family was under stress again. Then Mr. Bhiku Salunke, a friend of my father a uncle to me, came like an angel into my life. He had seen me working very hard and extended his help. My father also had helped him 18 years back to open a Credit Society from his commercial shop. Now my father is also a Director in the same Ashirwad Co-op Credit Society. He told me to open a T-shirt selling boutique and invested in me seven lacs. I could pay off many people and then started focusing on my boutique. But the story was no different, as the unsold stock was not helping in any case. I got convinced that I was lacking in experience in the retail business. I didn't have money to burn on promotions and inventory, and I wouldn't justify taking this loan. I decided to close this venture. I realized I didn't have a partner and was doing everything on my own, which was not the way to do business. The e-commerce space was starting then, and I couldn't capitalize on it due to a lack of funds, expertise, and human resources.

My father again stepped in and helped me with the balance money to be paid to Mr. Bhiku Salunke. He had received this money from selling a property my father had bought as an investment in my hometown. I used to constantly think about how my father helped me with his provident fund money and now with this sale of property amount also. My elder brother also criticized me for my failures.

This challenging period continued for a few months until I got a job at Paperboat Communications in Thane. I worked there for a few months, paid off a few more debts, and things settled down slowly. Every Sunday was a nightmare for me. There used to be constant discussions about my failures at home. I used to sit alone on the terrace and wonder how I would get back on track. My school friends Deepak Poptani and Maninder Singh Munde were around, but I couldn't reach out to them again and again. They had already helped me many times in the past. I was depressed and had a very tough time passing those days.

I started writing small format content and captions on Facebook during this time. These were all about motivational quotes. I gathered myself, and the fighter in me again used to motivate me. I was not the one to give up no matter what. I feel very nostalgic when Facebook sends us memories occasionally, but thinking of those times gives me shivers.

In about four months, I got a call from my mentor Abhay again, who offered me a job. I was delighted with the fact that I would be able to work with him, who was always supporting and understanding me. It was here I met my Vidula. She was very understanding and could see my struggle. She once saw someone asking for money from me and extended her help. She helped me financially also. Vidula is one of the strongest pillars in my life. I got attracted to her, and before we both realized it, we were in love with each other.

A big turn also came when I got a job in Nepal. I was desperate to earn money to pay off my debts. The salary was good, and I worked there for a few months. They used to pay us inconsistently and mostly in cash which didn't help me because I wanted to send the money back to India. This continued for a few months until I realized I could not stay away from Vidula and my parents.

I returned to India and got a job in Reliance, where I worked for a year. I told my parents about Vidula and expressed my desire to marry her. There was some opposition, but finally, everything fell in place, and we got married in February 2014. After a year, I was blessed with a beautiful daughter, whom we named Honeysha.

Vidula also had that spark in her for an entrepreneurial stint. She finally told me that she wanted to quit her job and would like to take up freelancing work. I was happy to hear this and encouraged her. My father was also equally supportive of this.

After about six months, Vidula realized she could not handle everything independently and needed support. Either someone else came on board, or I was always there to take the plunge. There were a lot of discussions at home. My father was petrified hearing I wanted to join a business again after my not-so-successful record but somewhere knew I was made for this only. We both showed him our promising business in hand, the clients ready to place their faith in us. He finally got convinced not before telling me that it is my life now, it is my family whom I need to work for, and the responsibilities and decisions I have to own going forward.

We got a small office for ourselves through one of our contacts from where we worked for a few months before we finally decided to rent a more prominent place. The business was getting better, clients appreciated our work, and we were getting good publicity through word-of-mouth.

One of my passions also lies in cycling. I'm a part of many cycle groups and have received recognition from France (BRM). Cycling has taught me a lot.

I participated in the annual 200Kms BRM night ride Mumbai-Kamshet (Near Lonavala)-Mumbai. I remember an incident when I reached Bhor ghat during the ride. There was a steep climb there, and we were already exhausted. After thinking and motivating each other, we could climb the road. I realized then the importance of how the mind plays a part in giving the right signals to the body. The muscles were tired, and the legs were aching, but the mind signalled the body to move on, and we could do it. This attitude is something I have imbibed more in myself. Not to give up, not to think negatively no matter what the situation or adverse the surrounding is.

Today, I'm proud that I have two offices, and twenty four people work for me. I was lucky to have met people like Farzana Suri, who have coached me to think differently and believe in myself. Farzana Suri is the reason for my second entrepreneurial journey. Without her one-on-one sessions, I wouldn't have begun again.

I'm also a BNI Gold member that has given me so much. I'm also an affiliate member of the Indian Institute of Interior Design.

* *

I realized then the importance of how the mind plays a part in giving the right signals to the body. The muscles were tired, and the legs were aching, but the mind signalled the body to move on, and we could do it. This attitude is something I have imbibed more in myself. Not to give up, not to think negatively no matter what the situation or adverse the surrounding is.

* *

Few more mentors who have contributed to my success are:

- Prem Jhangiani - my first boss at Beyond & Design. He taught me diplomacy and the shrewdness which is required in business. He was very inspirational.

- Abhay Lutade - a friend, philosopher, and guide. I always feel he knows more about me than what I do.

- Rajiv Talreja - Business Coach and a significant influencer who gave me the direction to scale my business. I learned from him to measure my potential clients - their needs, their desire, and understand their problems, after which winning them gets easy.

- Today we focus on the below sectors for our business generation, bringing architecture into reality.

    - Real Estate

    - Architects

    - Infrastructure

    - Roads

- Flyovers
- Interior Designing
- Healthcare & Pharma
- Financial sector
- Hotels & Resorts

From a humble background, struggling childhood, confused early years, and repeated mistakes that I've made to finally reaching the stability phase, I'm now on the threshold to growing exponentially.

Contents

The Million Dollar Question Always

What's your price?

"Understand there is a price to be paid for achieving anything of significance. You must be willing to pay the price"

John Wooden

This price question is hardly surprising. Imagine when you get that potential client calling you for a meeting. You prepare, set the PowerPoint presentation, organize the links to your work on social media, etc., and arrive at the client's office.

The meeting goes like this - blame the traffic, complain about the weather, sip water, and look around the office;

the client starts briefing even before exchanging the visiting cards. The client talks about his plans for the project he is working on, which goes on for some time. You start thinking about what great vision, what grand goals, and the budget must be enormous. You finally get an opportunity to talk, and before you start, the client hits you where it hurts the most – "give me a good price, okay." It doesn't stop there. "We have many projects coming up, so I expect you to work on this on a wafer-thin budget, and you will keep getting many opportunities from us." A carrot every now and then comes your way.

You also get calls from all your efforts in sales, digital marketing, and social media promotions. The phone rings and the person asks, "we heard about your company, saw your posts on social media, got your emails."

Hold your breath; the next question you hate to hear is, "what is your price? Do you have a rate card"? Unbelievable but true.

Do I hear you laugh? Does this connect with you?

Well, you gather all your courage, get that artificial smile on your face again and give a short overview of what you are, what you do, and how you do it. The client does not listen with great attention when you meet them in person, and you want to scream and tell them - listen to me, but it doesn't work like that.

****

The phone rings and the person asks, "we heard about your company, saw your posts on social media, got your emails." Hold your breath; the next question you hate to hear is, "what is your price? Do you have a rate card"? Unbelievable but true.

****

Does this tell us that it's all about price?

You will want your client to evaluate so many aspects before coming to a price that is undoubtedly important.

If I were my potential customer, I would want to assess my vendor in this form:

- See my work
- Visit my website

- Visit my social media pages
- Hear what other clients have to say about my work.
- ...and then call or invite us to your office.
- Assess my quality of work, team, experience, dedication, and consistent performance.
- But it doesn't happen like that.

Unfortunately, we cannot blame anyone; the industry has been spoilt for various reasons. When service is commoditized, this is bound to happen. Branding, positioning, credibility, and consistent performance matter a lot. Would we ever go to a five-star hotel and worry about why a dal-makhani is so expensive there vis-à-vis near our local restaurant? What are you paying for - yes, it is the experience, the ambience, the service, the brand, satisfying your ego, and many more things.

Service is such an essential element in our business. Even otherwise, we want good service. We go to a good restaurant, a movie hall, catch a flight, and hire a cab. Everywhere, besides its core promise, which is expected to be delivered, we want to be taken care of, attended to, listened to, and experience some unique service, after which we judge and say "the service was excellent."

Haven't we said after disembarking from a flight that the "service was good" and not that the plane landed minutes before its committed time. What are we eventually impressed with? Yes, it's service.

Ideally, we try and want to answer our clients in the below manner when they ask us a price to be quoted even before they know us well:

- We would be happy to hear about the project.
- We would love to get access to their drawings and files. Agreed, we are not selected yet at that stage, but the clients who have shared these with us have managed to get a reasonable price from us and many more things.
- We would want them to visit our social media pages and our website, which has so much in store to assess us thoroughly. Give us a reference from the posts or information we've uploaded, and then ask, "we liked this; how much did that cost to your customer." Ah! Now we

are talking.

If none of the above is possible, we love to hear what budget they have or are willing to spend. We can then indicate a range and specify that we have a limit below which we will not go down.

A relationship has to be a win-win. You win, we win, but it cannot be you win, and I lose, or I win, and you lose.

If price is the only criteria for selection, then you have not given anything else to your customer that he values. We at Weaverbird have gone out of our way to ensure our clients get immense value, excellent service, and quality of work. We have many stories where we have gone out of our way to ensure schedules are met, and expectations are surpassed. One way to back this up is to see our repeat business ratio. Today we have over 80% of our clients once on board coming back to us consistently.

To end on a cliché, I wonder if Shah Jahan had asked for the lowest quote for making the Taj Mahal.

But who knows....

Here's a glimpse of how transparent we are in our pricing intent. This chart is published on our website:

Weaverbird

Product/Service	Timeframe	Price Range
3D Ext Bungalow 	3-6 days per image	Rs 8000 - 25000 $300 - $850 for Intl
3D Residential Interior 	2-6 days per image	Rs 6000 - 10000 $150 - $350 for International clients
3D Ext Buildings 	4-6 days per image	Rs 15000 - 45000 $500 - $1250 for International clients
3D Commercial Interior 	4-6 days per image	Rs 8000 - 20000 $200 - $450 for International clients
3D Walkthrou Animation 	2-4 weeks	Rs 100,000 - 200,000 per min $2500 - $4500 per min for Intl
3D Product Rendering 	2-4 days per product	Rs 3000 - 20000 $150 - $450 for International clients
3D Floor Plans	3-4 Days	Rs 5000 - 25000

Note: Actual cost will be provided after checking autocad drawings.
Kindly drop a email: info@weaverbird.co.in or watsapp **+91 85911 44385** to arrange a 15 mins free zoom/google meet call.

* * *

Our Team Is Our Strength

What's your team strength?

"Great things in business are never done by one person. They are done by a team of people."

Steve Jobs

The world has changed all these years, especially after Covid-19. People do business with people, not with their office or their location. Deliverables, especially in the case of the service industry like us, matter the most once the expectations are set. The client doesn't mind even if you are sitting on a mountaintop as long as you are accessible, responsive and meeting the deadlines. We are no different.

Having said the above, we are a team of 35 people, including our team members, associates, partners, a panel of experts we hire project to project etc. This mix is a team which has taken me a lot of time to set. They have been handpicked, groomed and now lead in their respective zones, delivering consistently.

We offer a highly open culture of working style. Work from home is quite regular. We encourage our team to live a healthy and happy life, inspire social gatherings and celebrations of all kinds in our office and even motivate them to travel. Ultimately, it is the mind we know is working for us and not the physical body every time. Creativity can only blossom when the mind is at its best.

We have a good mix of people - from 3D artists, visualizers, animators, post-production team, photoshop specialists, copywriters, content writers, developers, client servicing executive, graphic team, sales & marketing team. The group is a perfect blend of vitality, youth, and experience and are leaders in their fields, with an average team member atleast having a two-year stint with us. This is not a bad start for a company that started six years back.

* *

Ultimately, it is the mind we know is working for us and not the physical body every time. Creativity can only blossom when the mind is at its best.

* *

I also pay a lot of attention to my team's training needs. Inviting industry leaders to my office is what we intend to practice often as ideas flow from all sides. Listening to practices and success stories from other industries also motivates everyone.

One interesting and vital aspect of my team strength is the culture we've set. We've put up a huge Charter or a Weaverbird Way of Working sheet in our reception area, which sets the tone when a client visits our office. The sheet explains what we are, how we are, and how we work and help anyone gauge our working culture.

The top qualities I look for in my team members include:

- Intensity - to work, perform, deliver

- Hunger - to succeed, to be ambitious

- Loyalty - towards the work and the Organization
- Integrity

We have a long way to go but I truly believe that my team and this working culture will take us places.

Here's the Culture Charter we have placed in our offices which just captures our DNA:

#weaverbirdculture

Weaverbird's Way

RELATION BECOMES RESISTANCE

NOT OUR WAY	SITUATION	OUR WAY
I know everything	EGO	I am open for suggestions
Don't care about fellow Collegues	NO BONDING	Co-operatives, helpful to the fellow collegues
Don't isolate anyone	GROUPISM	Be a part of the organisation
Don't talk to third person about any problem	BACK BITCHING	Talk to that person directly and clear all the doubts
I Don't care of the treating	SUPERIORITY	Treat everyone good and make a strong connection

#weaverbirdculture

Weaverbird's Way

ENERGY GOES DOWN

NOT OUR WAY	SITUATION	OUR WAY
I will take entire credit of my junior & associate work	**LACK OF APPRECIATION**	Appreciate other on all the aspects
Handeling work without even knowing what is the work in the hand	**OVER WORKD LOAD**	Ask for the work & then assigning work step by step
I will be just a part of that particular job	**FREEDOM OF AUTHORITY**	Take the responsibility of work by own and make the best of it
Showing feeling of unwarranted importance out of overbearing pride	**BEING ARROGANT TO OTHER**	Choosing word wisely before you say/using it

#weaverbirdculture

Weaverbird's Way

COMMITMENT IS CONDITIONAL

NOT OUR WAY	SITUATION	OUR WAY
Assigning any job before knowing the Interest and ask for it to happen	**ASSIGNING UNNECESSARY WORK**	Figure out the Interest and then assign the work for an effective result
Not allow space to show the creativity or the talent which one has.	**NO WORKFREE SPACE**	Give space and see what potential one can have to use all creativity

PERFORMANCE FILLED WITH REASON

NOT OUR WAY	SITUATION	OUR WAY
Pushing to any work which he/she not that well trained	**NOT INTERESTED IN WORK GIVEN**	Ask about particular work then only assign it

* * *

Our Geographical Presence

Where Is Your Office Located?

"Geography is History"

Iridium - Satellite Telephone Service promoted

by Motorola

Geography is indeed history now. Just as how it doesn't matter where your team operates from, it equally doesn't matter where your office is. Get your business asset-light, and what better strategy than not having a physical office justifies this. Well, we have our base in Mulund, Mumbai, but with each passing day, we are experiencing it being used less. The team works from home, sometimes from a Café, and I'm constantly on the move. But we all are bound and connected with technology. Coming to the office is an event now. Unless there's a client visit, I don't visit the office.

Besides Mumbai, we have invested and focused in tier two and three cities. Nasik, which is hardly two hours from Mumbai, is another strategically important market for us. Several projects are coming up there, and we've made some significant inroads also. It will predominantly be a sales and customer service office, with all execution work handled from Mumbai.

Next on our planning sheet is a joint venture we are entering with a Kolkata & Ahmedabad-based company. Then there is Dubai which is another huge market for us. We've also started looking at London to have a base, and somewhere in quarter two of the year 2022, we should be launching our office there.

With a global client base, from Mexico, Sweden, and Dubai to Canada, we hope to consolidate our presence in our carefully selected markets.

I'm thoroughly enjoying this growth phase we've entered. I see the impetus further by remaining nimble, strategically outsourcing non-core activities, being asset-light and nurturing my team.

* * *

The Software Applications We Use

Our Tools

"Styles come and go. Good design is a language not a style"

by Massimo Vignelli, Designer

Technology has simplified processes and our lives, and who can deny this. For someone like us, where software applications play a crucial role, the most significant benefit has been the ability to transform our ideas into reality, thanks to the various software available and the ones we use.

Today, file storage is another area which has made accessibility a non-existent issue. Remember the times of corrupt devices, hard drives not having enough storage capacity etc. Cloud-based storage has helped massively further as we deal with cumbersome files.

Here's a list of the 3D Software and Plugins we regularly use:

- ZBrush
- SketchUp
- Auto cad
- Autodesk 3ds Max
- Autodesk Maya
- Cinema 4D
- Blender
- Rhinoceros 3D Element 3D
- K-3D
- Lumion
- Autodesk Revit
- ArchiCAD
- V-Ray

- Corona
- Mental ray
- Unreal Engine

Creation is one part, but the rendering process is equally crucial. For rendering, we primarily use V-Ray, Lumion, Blender and Corona as our engines.

The configuration of our workstations are as follows:

Processor: 11th Gen Intel® Core™ i9 - 11900K @3.50GHz

Motherboard: INTEL 560MDS3H / Wi–Fi / BT

RAM: 32GB DDR4 Ram XPG 3200

HardDisk: 500GB NVMe + 1 TB SATA HDD

Graphic Card: Nvidia GeForce 3060 - 12GB Graphic Card

750W 80 plus Modular Power Supply unit

Dell FHD 24inch, Keyboard & Mouse

UPS 3550 APC 600 va

We use Render farm to complete the rendering process. We have our server where we eventually save the heavy files with a six months parking space for each of our clients, after which we free it.

* * *

The Schedules

The Timeframes We Work On

"The key is not to prioritize what's on your schedule, but to schedule your priorities"

Stephen Covey

Anyone from the service industry will tell you that giving a schedule is one of the most challenging things. Very seldom can the service provider mention that their deliverables depend upon how I receive the inputs from their client's side?

We are no different but do our best to work proactively.

Here's how we do it...

On a good day, we get a call from our clients, saying, "The

files are ready; start working on these, and I hope to hear from you in the next three to four days. If you have any approvals or questions, do not hesitate to call me anytime. This project is a priority, and we will respond immediately as our deadline is clear".

Wow! This conversation makes us feel it is an excellent client. Do you know why? Because the client has conveyed to us the end date and has understood how this process works.

But what is the reality? Everything was required yesterday, and the files will come tomorrow.

Follow-up is one of the biggest industries, and we experience this repeatedly.

We have some great clients on board. Over time, they have understood how we work, the SOPs we follow, the culture charter I mentioned earlier, and most importantly, they have experienced us. Most of the time, we work on a schedule with the end date in mind. We expect a one-point contact for approvals, and everything falls in place.

****

Follow-up is one of the biggest industries and we experience this repeatedly.

****

All that is in control of us is taken care of, but we have to handle uncertainties. We understand that sometimes there are things which are beyond anyone's control. Still, ideally, all external approval points, such as architects, also need to fall in sync with the eventual deadline or the schedule goes off-track completely.

It all starts with the AutoCAD file we receive as our inputs. Once we study this, it becomes relatively easier to predict the scope of work and the time we will take to deliver.

It will be interesting for the reader to know that some projects get completed in less than a week, and there are a few which take ages for various reasons.

Here are a few top reasons for the delays:

- Incorrect input AutoCAD files

- Lack of clarity on the expectations
- No set priorities for completion
- Delay or slow responses in approvals
- Too much co-ordination internally or with external associates for decision making.

We always tell our clients that no matter what the project is, what revenue we are getting from it or for whom the work is being delivered, our efforts, time to be taken on it, and the labour involved will not change with the intensity not being compromised at all.

When the great singer Kishore Kumar sang a song, did he compromise on his voice quality and delivery depending upon which movie it was for, the actor he was singing for or, for that matter, what amount he was getting paid? Of course not, and that is why we see some marvellous gems from the great Kishore for top musicians and less acclaimed artists.

* * *

Which Clients Do You Work With?

Our client list

"A satisfied customer is the best business strategy of all"

Michael LeBoeuf

As they say, it takes a lot of time to win a new good customer, but it takes a few seconds to lose one. We all read books, educate ourselves, and listen to the best professionals to deeply understand how to grow business, win new clients, set up a lead magnet, master social media marketing, etc., but the good old strategy remains unchanged. A satisfied customer gets you business repeatedly. He becomes your voice to attract new customers, refers to many, understands your working pattern, and doesn't pull you down on prices. He is always a great advocate for your business. Nothing works better than a recommendation or a testimonial from a satisfied customer.

We are incredibly proud of how we've handled our clients and are truly blessed to have some excellent names on our list. We've not only focused on our strengths but also tried the untested to push ourselves on what we can deliver. Hence, this is only expanding our client base over these years.

Focus works brilliant for our team, and learning the art of saying "No" has been appreciated by our clients. It's always good to deliver what we can rather than experiment and lose potential projects and that client forever.

Broadly, the real estate, infrastructure and hospitality sectors have been our strengths. Still, over these years, we've seen a growing number of industries also wanting our services for promoting their business, such as banking & finance, pharma and the manufacturing industry in general. Compared to a still picture, an animated 3D rendered one will always be attractive.

Here's a glimpse on our client base:

Real Estate:

1. Spark Developers
2. Parksyde Jaikumar Constructions, Nashik
3. Bora Realty, Pune
4. Panvelkar Group
5. Punir Gaurav Developers
6. Sri Group
7. Sunrise Housing Constructions
8. RRC Ventures
9. Indu Enterprises, Bilaspur Chattisgarh

10. Shrinath Realty, Nashik

11. Shapoorji Pallonji

12. House of Hiranandani

Resorts & Hotels:

1. Intocada Realtors LLP

2. Punir Gaurav Resorts

Infrastructure:

1. Samkit Engineers - KDMC

2. Punir Gaurav Cruises

3. Kalyan Dombivli Municipal Corporation

Over 100 Architects & Interior Designers

* * *

Do You Make Elevations?

A little more on our scope of work

"The difference between where you are now and where you will get to later defines your range of work which you have to be responsible for"

Israelmore Ayivor

To answer this question to the point: No, we don't make elevations.

But as a boutique 3D-Visualization firm, we get these requests from various clients. The elevation is a creative thought process delivered primarily by architects. A lot of brainstorming goes into this, and very rightly so. The exterior of the project defines the elevation and is the most attractive part of the creation.

When we get these requests, we utilize our panel of architects from whom we get this done and deliver it to the client.

Another continuation of a service request from our client is when we are asked to make the drawings. We cannot blame the clients for these requests but here again, it is the primary responsibility of the architects who deliver these, and it is an extension of the elevations only.

Some enterprising clients also want us to recce. In simple terms "the process of visiting and quickly looking around a place to find out information about it". Our work starts when we get the drawings from our clients, and there's no need to visit the sites. Still, sometimes it gets crucial as it is vital to know the surroundings of the projects, the soil around, and the landscape next to it as everything needs to fall in place properly. We do adhere to these requests depending upon various parameters.

My passion for my business also helps me visit places far and wide. I find myself lucky to be in this business, which sometimes takes me to the site of places I wouldn't have dreamt of otherwise. Visiting various locations of Maharashtra, Chattisgarh, Goa, Gulbarga in Karnataka,

Seaports, Navy base in Vizag etc., would be unimaginable. Still, thanks to my core function for doing recce, we get these opportunities, and I truly love and value that. We have also observed that clients appreciate our visit and realize how serious we are in our work.

****

My passion for my business also helps me visit places far and wide. I find myself lucky to be in this business, which sometimes takes me to the site of places I wouldn't have dreamt of otherwise.

****

Finally, the clients also ask us to help them with the measurements of their projects. Again, we are not experts in this, but all the above requests come up as clients want solutions coming from a single point of contact, and we see this as a moment of faith put in by our clients. We normally again outsource this work to our panel of surveyors who deal with our clients directly.

***

Why do you think we should give you work?

What makes us standout vis-à-vis competition?

"The most essential quality for leadership is not perfection
but
credibility. People must be able to trust you"

Rick Warren

How many of us get this question from our prospective customers: Why should we give you the work, what are your differentiators, what makes you unique, and why should we select you over our proven and tested supplier or vendor who is associated with us all these years?

Somewhere deep down, the fact is, the customer knows his existing vendor has let him down, or he is exploring a new one to get some fresh ideas. There has to be some reason, and before taking the plunge, he asks this hard-hitting question to test how such a question will be answered in the first place. If the first step itself is not responded well, if one doesn't get a foot in the door, one cannot proceed ahead.

Here are a few top reasons why a client should work with us:

- We weave client stories, ideas & designs most creatively and elegantly possible. We not only do work randomly, but we also provide clients with well-planned 3D renderings and animations, which eventually generate more bookings than they usually get on their projects.

- We not only deliver or hand over work to clients as per contract or scope of work while signing an agreement. We go that extra mile and provide additional work/services to clients, which makes them overwhelmed because they get unexpected jobs which were never discussed. An example is offering two or three short 3D rendering walkthrough videos, which they can also use for social media like Instagram, Facebook and WhatsApp promotions.

- We offer clients an efficient and straightforward approach by listening to their ideas. If required, we suggest our thoughts on new concepts and deliverables. Sometimes we have even saved some extra cost that was not necessary for the project.

- While working on the client's projects, we grasp the image that the client has envisaged in their mind and help them to transform the same into reality. Our clairvoyant approach and diligence make every client for any amendment or modifications required once the 3D output is ready.

- Punctuality, meticulous attention to every detail of a project, co-ordination, approachability, professionalism and fastest delivery make us different from others.

- Before initiating the work, we sit with clients and explain our process of work step by step and make them comfortable to establish the right working environment with my team. I think the expectations here get set effectively, which helps both the client and us to work as per desired schedules agreed mutually.

- Finally, we ask these simple questions to gain clarity and fully justify our work:

- ✓ What are your exact needs, desires & pain points?
- ✓ What is the solution that can help you ease your pain point?
- ✓ Which quality and style offered to you would be most comfortable?

We take pride in our work and the way we deliver. No matter what and how much we say, the reality can only be conveyed by an existing customer and here are a few testimonials which speak everything:

- ❖ "Weaverbird truly weaves a brand story most creatively and elegantly possible. They provided us with well-planned animation videos, which helped us to reach out to our prospects. They generated 28% more business than we usually do. I must say that their strategizing and execution is par excellence."

Vinod Tejwani – Managing Director, Pranda Jewellery India.

- "Our journey with Weaverbird started two years back. They are an extremely talented team to work with in terms of 3D renderings. Punctuality and fastest delivery are what make them different from others. We have worked with several freelancers and small studios, but Weaverbird has taught us the meaning of professionalism. My best wishes to Weaverbird."

  Arpit Chopda - Sales & Marketing Head, Sunrise Developers.

- "I got an opportunity to work with Weaverbird and the team recently for one of my project presentations for a multipurpose commercial project for creating a 3D-walkthrough animation. I must say I am impressed by their ability to grasp the image I had envisaged in my mind, which helped me transform the same into reality. Their clairvoyant approach and the diligence with which their team welcomed my request for amendment is commendable. They managed to complete my work within the short period possible.

The 3D elevation looks superb; their team is amazing, with meticulous attention to every detail and understanding of the needs. Super job indeed!!!. Thanks once again, and keep designing such timeless pieces of art. All the best".

Architect Sunil Thanawala - Plain Arch Associates.

****

Weaverbird Process of Work for 3D Renderings:

1. Technical meeting with the client.

2. We conduct the technical meeting with the client to understand cad drawings (briefing from the client)

3. Work Initiating

4. If anything is missing, we request the client to send it across. Once we receive everything, we initiate the work only after that.

5. Grey Renderings - First Cut

6. Initially, we share as a grey rendered / screenshot for approval for structure, materials, textures, and camera angles.

7. Test Renderings - Second Cut

8. After approval on grey renderings we share test rendered using materials, textures, colour combinations etc (second cut/preview)

9. Final HD - Final Cut

After approval on grey renderings, we share test rendered using materials, textures, colour combinations etc (second cut/preview)

Normally, we entertain two rounds of changes. If additional changes are required after the two rounds, extra cost is added (mentioned already in contract also)

Assumptions:

1. This agreement is based on the architectural and Interior AutoCAD files. e.g. AutoCAD DWG file provided by the client.

2. Changes will be made twice as per requirement; Any additional changes will cost extra.

3. Any services performed for the client by Weaverbird on the project defined herein in place of an executed agreement shall constitute an implied acceptance by the client for the scope, fees, and terms defined herein for those services rendered.

Information to be provided by the client:

1. The name and position of a single representative who will have the authority to accept and approve the services and invoices provided by the Weaverbird to direct tasks as per contract on behalf of the client or Owner.

2. AutoCAD drawings (floor plans and elevations)

3. References (Materials, Textures, Style)

4. Images, Pictures of Product

5. Camera angles for 3D exterior image only

6. Project highlights

7. Video script/narration (Only if its Walkthrough)

8. Flow of the video which you're expecting (Only if its Walkthrough)

9. Project's Google location

* * *

Do You Take Small Value Projects?

What Is Our Per Project Bandwidth Of Revenue?

"Great things are done by a series of small things brought together."

Vincent Van Gogh

Every business, you will agree, has a finite resource. No matter how much one aspires to grow with existing resources, one knows that you cannot deliver and meet customer expectations after a point. The earlier you realise this, the better it is, or you end up biting more than what you can chew. Time is the biggest constraint – not your ability, energy, or expertise. All these are manageable to some extent, or you can get external help or outsource. But what do we do on the time element?

Hence, in creative fields like ours, we cannot deliver less for a small sum agreed upon compared to projects where we get paid justifying our time, efforts and all resources. We always strive to provide the best.

But to service a range of requests we get, we have simplified the conversion and deliverables to suit every pocket by way of resources we allocate. The Key account management models (KAM) we've internally set deliver on a template-based model requiring the least of our time, etc. This way, we are in a position to cater to a larger group of customers, ideally addressing all pocket budgets.

The critical aspect which drives us is that our current biggest customer was small once upon a time too. We love to engage with our clients in their projects as trustworthy partners and like to grow with them. Then there are decisions we take as any other prudent businessman would take. We value our involvement, efforts, and overall timelines and package our commercials accordingly.

* * *

Can you match my lowest bid received?

How Competitive Can We Get To Acquire New Business?

"Good work ain't cheap, ...Cheap work, ain't good"

Norman "Sailor Jerry" Collins

One last point of discussion is how competitive we are, sometimes, despite customers getting convinced we are their right choice. It's a hyper-competitive world, and we all are spoilt on choice. But is the lowest price the best? Of course not, and we all know that.

In a race to win projects irrespective of any industry, there will always be one vendor with the lowest price. But does that mean they are the best on all fronts? It can be a wrong calculation or estimation of the work involved. Would you like to work with a consistent, trustworthy vendor, or would you prefer someone uncertain on all fronts? Do you like surprises to pop up later as a price escalation?

We get these requests when our prospective customer asks us to match the price. Here again, it is our call. We may have had a good time with this client since the time this request came in. We usually assess the situation as the right to reject or accept a project is also with us. Just as clients judge us on quality, price, schedule and experience, we place our judgement on the below:

- Will the customer fit our culture?
- How clear are our goal posts?
- Are the expectations in sync?
- Is there a long-term prospect?
- What value can we get from this association if the customer comes on board? Better brand image for

us, credibility, resource, prestige or is it simply high-ticket value?

Even if we have to take a hit on our revenue, we may decide to match customer expectations if an inner voice tells us to do so. We love to win good customers, not just current transactions.

As Benjamin Franklin said "the bitterness of poor quality remains long after the sweetness of low price is forgotten".

We eye long-term relationships. We always make it a point to convey to the client that we will agree to match their current low price received but would always look at the next project, which also needs to come to us on our legitimate terms.

We understand there's price, performance and delivery pressure to all and are happy to collaborate with clients with whom we can travel the distance.

* *

In a race to win projects irrespective of any industry, there will always be one vendor with the lowest price. But does that mean they are the best on all fronts?

* *

* * *

Some Rapid-Fire Questions We Usually Get

Temptations are many.

"Focus is a matter of deciding what things you're not going to do"

John Carmack

In almost every conversation, clients usually ask these questions some time or the other. There are temptations to say yes, but over a while, we've resisted them to stay focused, and that's how we've got the desired mileage despite a lot of low-hanging fruits always around us. Clients also appreciate this as the ability and courage to say "No" to a client is not with many.

Here are a few frequently asked questions to us:

- Do you offer generic designing services other than 3D rendering?

- How tempting this is. We have our in-house team of graphic designers, and we can always say a big yes to this. Still, we know we will eventually become a graphic designing company. While we understand where the client comes from, we have to answer this strategically by mentioning that we can do this only for the Real estate and, in the case of the Infrastructure industries only. What good this does to us is that our positioning doesn't hamper, and it becomes more of an extension or supplementing services to the same client where our focus is. Hence, besides 3D rendering, clients are also happy to know that we can design their brochures, leaflets, and posters for the project we have undertaken.

- Can you send your person on-site? Let them camp on our premises, and we can expedite the work?

- To please our clients, here again, there's a temptation to say yes. Accepting this also can be in our interest as the projects can end faster for us with quick co-ordination and decisions. But once we say yes, imagine multiple clients asking for this. We will end up having an empty office and more people on-site. Employees also need those breaks to switch on and off, which they can do sitting in our own office, not full-time at the client's office. Hence, we have to reject this request.

- How can we pay you in advance? We are not a Mumbai based firm where you are - how would this work if you don't deliver?

This question would carry a lot of weight till about ten years back, not now, especially post-Covid; this question is irrelevant.

The world outsources to countries where the back-end and manufacturing are miles apart. A US company focuses on branding and marketing with all manufacturing and customer support based in either China or India, as an example. With technology entering almost every industry and business - may it be for products or services; this question is already answered.

But some companies still have these doubts. A company based in Hyderabad asked us this question recently. To ensure we both get comfortable, we tell them to issue a proper work order or a purchase order duly signed and stamped by the highest authority. The practice of insisting on an advance payment applies to every client of ours irrespective of their geographical location.

In this virtual world, geography is history now.

- Do you do Scripting and Voiceover?

- This is a significant value-add we enjoy doing also. This request also indicates the faith shown in our abilities and services. When a client asks something like this, it shows that our core work of 3D rendering is already appreciated. Now, the client wants more from us and is looking at us as a one-stop for them. Again, though not our core work, we enjoy doing this because of the fantastic panel we have in the back-end.

- Do you do drone shoots?

- There was a time when this was the in thing. The technology was new, the players were not many, and the cameras were not ready, but now the scene was different. With multiple players offering this service and a few doing fantastic in their chosen field, we've consciously slipped out of this. But we do offer our clients our support to get one on board. It's a win-win for all and helps to add value in any case.

- Do you do Digital Marketing?

- Again, a massive temptation, but we stay out of this. The client thinks we've created their work and can quickly market these on social media, but that is a specialized field again. The power of focus comes into the picture here. Hence, we help our clients to a good Digital Marketing agency we know to progress ahead.

- Do you negotiate or is this your fixed price?

- In a service industry like ours, where creativity, art, and visual imagination matter, a price cannot be fixed. We don't sell a product. If we were selling toothpaste, it would cost the same in a departmental store, a hyper-food mall or even a nearby local store. The customer would not pay a premium anywhere.

But we are open to discussions. While we try to unturn every stone before giving a price, we often realize that client expectations and deliverables are different - sometimes fundamental. Hence, we love to get into discussions and more briefings so that the same goal post is clear to both and the client receives value for money. The point here is not to over-charge or under-charge but to value our work appropriately. Once we get the proper drawings, the pricing becomes more real.

- Do you work on Saturdays and Sundays?

- We value our employees, their private life, and the work-life balance they need. Especially in a creative field such as ours, a relaxed and happy mind can give spectacular results vis-à-vis a stressed one. We work alternate Saturdays, and Sundays are fully closed. Still, we do understand, and if the situation demands, our team will deliver on these days also. This flexibility is crucial for clients to know how sensitive we are to meeting their objectives.

- If I send you a CAD drawing which includes the plans and elevations along with the scope of work, will you be able to tell us a price?

This is the ideal customer to talk to us in this manner. This clarity helps us to quote most appropriately. To come on the same wavelength, meet expectations, benefit mutually and operate as a partnering model rather than a vendor/

client model, such communication is what we love. This conversation eases expectations, and goals get set very nicely. Especially when someone asks such a question, we know the client is professional and knows how to get the best out of us, saving time, money and energy.

Our industry needs this change. The perspective needs to change to grow altogether. Gone are the days when clients squeezed everything out of their vendors, and the price was the only differentiating factor. Today, price, quality and delivery are presumed to be in place. To give spectacular results, clients need to work with service providers like us effectively, offering empathy, understanding of challenges faced and setting reasonable goals to work from a long-term point of view.

As the client expects clarity from their clients, so is the case with us. Ultimately, we need to treat the vendor the way you would want to be treated by your customer also.

****

Our industry needs this change. The perspective needs to change to grow altogether. Gone are the days when clients squeezed everything out of their vendors, and the price was the only differentiating factor.

****

- How many team members do you have in 3D modelling, rendering, post-production and project managers?

- Clients are very keen to know the team structure and the configuration. To a large extent, the client is testing if we are a company with proper systems, procedures, team etc. or are we a freelancer or a small company with an outsourcing model primarily used for deliverables. We feel happy when the client asks this question to us before we can convey it.

Here's our team configuration:

- Modelling - 9
- Rendering - 4
- Post-production - 3

- Project Managers - 3
- Accounts -1
- Marketing - 2
- Sales - 2

Then we have associates all over India who work with us on a project basis, but they are dedicated to us every time.

The idea is to run a professional set-up with clarity of roles & responsibilities so that the deliverables are met correctly. This team structure gives our clients confidence to see we have back-ups to ensure the continuity of work remains at any point in time. Clients do not like to hear that "our designer is not well or is on leave", because of which there will be a delay or we've lost the files and will have to re-create them to deliver. Such uncertainties do not help, which has been a great differentiator in our business.

****

The idea is to run a professional set-up with clarity of roles & responsibilities so that the deliverables are met correctly.

****

- Do you conduct online meetings also?

This may appear a straightforward question, and we realize it is more of fear from the client's side. We love doing this as it saves time and travel costs, but clients are often unsure of their schedules. They give us a specific day and time but are not present. It's a complete waste of time. Some crucial meetings are required to be done in person, and we insist on that. Still, once the process and understanding are set, it becomes wonderful to work online with the entire team contributing to the meeting rather than just one or two attending the same.

Since we also work on a global scale, post-Covid, it has helped us conduct as many online meetings as possible to maximize our deliverables faster.

- Are you aware of technical drawings, or shall I speak to your technical team?

This question is taken for granted most of the time. Clients should not take it for granted that the person from our firm who is in touch with them in acquiring the business is also equipped to handle technical questions. As an entrepreneur,

I'm running a business; I'm not a freelancer or a solopreneur. We have a well-structured team that has clear strengths, roles and responsibilities.

In his book "Good to Great", Jim Collins said " First Who ... Then What. We expected good-to-great leaders to begin by setting a new vision and strategy. Instead, we found that they got the right people on the bus, the wrong people off the bus, and the right people in the right seats—and then they figured out where to drive it. The old adage "People are your most important asset" turns out to be wrong. People are not your most important asset. The right people are."

Source: https://www.jimcollins.com/article_topics/articles/good-to-great.html

This masterpiece from Jim Collins sums up how we have configured our team, and we put the right people for the right job. Clients also do not like to hear "I will get back to you". They do not want to hear "let me discuss with the technical team and revert" or "I'm not the right person to discuss this" after spending time on the inputs received. Ideally, when there are technical discussions, we ensure our technical person only discusses. This approach ensures everyone is on the same page and the desired results are achieved quickly.

****

As an entrepreneur, I'm running a business; I'm not a freelancer or a solopreneur. We have a well-structured team that has clear strengths, roles and responsibilities.

****

- Can you give me good quality results irrespective of the software you use?

Ah! It is a seasoned question coming from someone who has known the trade for a long-time. In today's challenging world of cost efficiency, which every client wants to achieve, everyone wants the best in the world at less price but without compromising on quality.

- But this remains a distant dream. Why would we pay more for an Apple phone compared to others?

It is the quality and technical configuration, but most importantly, it is also the experience as you want to flaunt with it now to make that impression. Can you give me good quality results irrespective of the software you use?

Our work is no different. Ours is an experiential brand where our work speaks for itself. While someone can have the best software in place, if technical strengths are missing, one cannot deliver. There is no other way around where you can deliver spectacularly with ordinary resources.

Having said this, we have the best software, as mentioned earlier, and the best people on the job. To simplify further and to meet a more extensive base of customers, we offer average, standard and premium output.

While the quality of work in terms of resolution will not suffer, the efforts and commitment will also not be compromised, which results into:

- Rendering, which may vary
- Photos may not look very realistic
- The post-production finish may come with minor detailing.

These expectations are well-accepted by clients. While we

go to explain the results beforehand, they know what they will get for the price they pay and for the time we will spend on it. As we are in the creative business, besides the actual project value, we have to value the time taken to complete it, for which the pricing varies vastly. Accordingly, we have to give the output also.

Before signing up the terms, the client also sends us inputs to look for the kind of work expected. Often it is here we know what kind of files are desired. Their preference, the work they have liked of ours from the past etc. It becomes easy for us to price their project as we know their expected results.

* *

As we are in the creative business, besides the actual project value, we have to value the time taken to complete it, for which the pricing varies vastly. Accordingly, we have to give the output also.

* *

- Do you accept advance? What are your terms?

Yes, this is a crucial part of signing the deal, and we insist on getting an advance. The release of advance gets seriousness in work from both sides. Broadly, our terms look like these:

- 30% advance on signing the deal

- 40% once we submit the first cut with a good look and feel.

- 30% once the final version is sent to the client with our watermark of a logo. This version is the final delivery, and to get the final high-resolution file; we expect the client to pay us this amount.

Let me also mention that an advance may not be possible with specific large clients or with Govt. organizations. Hence, in such cases, we insist on a work order or a purchase order with all terms duly captured.

- Do you have any commercial terms or agreements in place?

- Our Commercial Agreement is a four-page document with complete clarity of inputs we need, the terms & conditions, the treatment we give to their files once the project is completed etc. It is crucial to set this in place. The client goes through this as this leaves no scope for ambiguity. The client sometimes gets carried away due to timelines pressure to complete the project quickly. Some vendors over-commit or promise unrealistically, but we don't. We've rejected projects due to unrealistic expectations as we believe in winning long-term relationships than winning only a transaction in the discussion. Ultimately, not all are your clients and the decision to accept or reject also lies with us.

****

The client sometimes gets carried away due to timelines pressure to complete the project quickly. Some vendors over-commit or promise unrealistically, but we don't.

****

- Do you have in-house render farms?

- A very straightforward question often asked to us. We don't have in-house but use the Chinese render farms to complete the tasks.

- Upon completion of the work, before publishing it on social media/websites, do you take permission from the client?

- Of course, we do. Without clients' permission on an email, we do not publish the work for any promotional and marketing purpose.

- My project is in London and Sweden, will you able work with people abroad in their time zones?

- A reality of today. All businesses are global, and sourcing from anywhere is common to almost all companies. We get such requests where the client has staff members abroad and want us to co-ordinate with them from here in India. We do align with the people abroad to find a sweet spot mutually. Our staff members work like in shifts to make sure communication and co-ordination don't suffer. Virtual offices and global staffing are a reality, with technology enabling this like never before.

* * *

A Million-Dollar Statement Made To Us

"I can give you the price you want but I cannot compromise on quality delivered to us"

"It's easier to explain price once than to apologize for quality forever"

Zig Ziglar

Wow! This price-quality statement can keep any entrepreneur going. As we know, an entrepreneur is not answerable to anyone except himself. These statements made by customers you meet occasionally drive you again and again. Such clients are what you work for, and these urge you indeed. It is challenging, pushes your limits, increases responsibilities, and makes you more accountable. This is when you need your team to perform above their potential, give their best and deliver to retain this client forever.

When we get such a customer, it just lifts our spirits. We know that this customer will be supportive. Such customers know the market and its players well. They understand how to extract the best from their vendors, give them a free hand, and be supportive and appreciative of their efforts. Still, the bottom line will be - he needs the best.

Just as service providers like us need consistency in business flow and good customers to establish a long-term partnering model, it is the same with customers. They, too, need reliable, trustworthy and consistent performers who will not let them down. This requirement is a brilliant relationship to enter with someone, and we thrive just as any other performer would. In the 80:20 ratio of anyone's client list, we've realised that most of the clients in the 20 percent are of this character.

Over these years, we've been fortunate to have found many who have had shades of such a character. They need good quality work and are happy to pay us on our expected legitimate terms, and the relationship has blossomed. This equation is the absolute win-win situation anyone would want to enter, based on trust and consistency in overall deliverables.

* *

Just as service providers like us need consistency in business flow and good customers to establish a long-term partnering model, it is the same with customers. They, too, need reliable, trustworthy and consistent performers who will not let them down.

* *

* * *

Common Negotiation & Persuasion Techniques

The good old carrot technique used.

"In a negotiation, we must find a solution that pleases everyone, because no one accepts that they must lose and that the other must win, both must Win!"

Nabil N Jamal

Here's something you would have heard from your customers:

- "Look, my budget is tight, so I won't be able to pay your price. Is it okay that you work at my price this time, and next time I'll work at your price?"
- We've fallen prey to this technique in our initial days

when we needed a good flow of regular work, but that "next time" never came. On the contrary, we were made to work on the same terms or lesser price again.

- "What if I assure you with certain work for next one year. Can you offer me a discounted price? We can enter into contracts if that works."
- This discussion always happens in thin air. It is always verbal - in person or on the phone but nothing on paper. The contracts are never made, and the commitments are never sent, even on an email when we insist. The "certain work" is not quantifiable or forecasted but is always mentioned as projects in the pipeline. Still, these so-called pipelines are only on paper with nothing concrete.
- "I will introduce you to a couple more builder clients with similar projects in a different location. Can you give me a discount on my next project?"

Such a statement is a powerful one and sounds very realistic. This establishes a sense of authority for the client in a discussion. Again, the referrals only come later once the project in hand is delivered, which to a great extent, we feel will speak for itself if we've done an excellent job.

Honestly, we know where the client is coming from and appreciate it. We understand they want to squeeze us but always wonder why? Ultimately, the projects are worth crores. Why would anyone want to squeeze a vendor who will help them portray the project in a manner that will only help the eventual objective in sales? Why turn your strength into your visible weakness? Again, would a creative person think less for less money or not deliver their best because a few thousand paid less? Doing so will only damage their reputation and credibility.

There was a time in the initial days of our business when we ignored and chose to fall prey to these techniques. We were desperate to build our portfolio but not anymore. We don't say this with any extent of arrogance or over-confidence. With experience and a belief that all appreciate our work, why compromise on our pricing, especially when we know that we are fair in what we are asking and will not leave any stone unturned to deliver spectacularly.

* *

Ultimately, the projects are worth crores. Why would anyone want to squeeze a vendor who will help them portray the project in a manner that will only help the eventual objective in sales? Why turn your strength into your visible weakness?

* *

* * *

The Advisory Role We Play

"A consultant to be worth his salt must give honest judgements not necessarily those which he thinks the client would like to hear!"

Andrew Thomas

Call it ignorance or innocence. We hear clients saying, "After seeing our cad drawings and project location, what do you think - which services will be relevant to me and my project from the services you offer?

This is a tricky situation, especially when the client is new to us and if the conversation is on the phone and not in person. One needs to understand if this question is to test us or if the client is ignorant or innocent about how to proceed.

Whatever the case, we look at this as an honest question and answer, being ruthlessly honest irrespective of the outcome. It is a part of our free consultancy or advisory role we play, having worked in this industry for a long-time. We are here to win long-term clients and relationships and not one-off transactions. The client can benefit and save money if we give the proper guidance by looking at their CAD drawings. My role and responsibilities are beyond business as I take great pride in grooming young students, and clients are no exception. Please visit www.vinodpatil.com, which is made from passion and love for my work.

I would never do anything to harm my reputation and personal brand. Such opportunities when the client asks for genuine help are the right platforms for me to strengthen my brand by offering the right advice.

****

My role and responsibilities are beyond business as I take great pride in grooming young students, and clients are no exception. Please visit www.vinodpatil.com, which is made from passion and love for my work.

****

***

My Stories & My Experience

"The key to success is to focus on goals not obstacles"

Unknown

Every day is a learning process. It is just the attitude you need to have - to stay hungry.

In all these years of building our business, I've come across some extraordinary people, situations and challenges that have only strengthened me. It was not easy initially, but eventually, we thrived on challenges. The joy of owning the challenge, working on options and giving results to clients beyond their expectations was unmeasurable.

Here are a few case studies which made us stronger.

Case Study: Punir Gaurav, Thane

About the company

Punir Gaurav is a project spread across 33 acres in the middle of the Raigarh district at Srivardhan. Amid an expansive land, giving a breath-taking sight surrounded by an abundance of greenery, the view will make you feel close to Mother Nature. Their motto is "Destination- Happiness', and the facilities they offer are an absolute delight. The core objective of the plan was to generate leads from the work they would allot to us, and subsequently, their sales team would take charge.

Challenges

While planning this project in mind, the client felt the need for an unusual way of showcasing their vision to the world. Several attempts were made, but none were up to the mark. They used to create small videos, photos of the place, and PowerPoint presentations to illustrate their work, but nothing worked in their favour. By the time they realized that instead of all the previous presentations, why not present it in 3D so that people could experience the view. They searched a lot of agencies for their needs, but none of them was under consideration. The magic of referrals and the power of word-of-mouth worked. The client approached us through a reference of a gentleman named Amey Katkar, owner of the Digital Marketing agency called 4P Solutions.

* *

The core objective of the plan was to generate leads from the work they would allot to us, and subsequently, their sales team would take charge.

* *

Solution

We started with online meetings for taking briefs since the client is Dubai based. The team started understanding their purpose of creating a 3D walkthrough and rendering images. The extensive discussion on video calls and time scheduling was always challenging. Gautam Pradhan, MD of the company, shared his vision and mission. Ideas were exchanged between the client regularly through emails. It was an experience, and we thoroughly enjoyed working on it.

We suggested to him that we should make a 3D rendering walkthrough, rendering images and Drone shoot since the project has a picturesque location, close to a beach, surrounded by mountains.

Result

After an intense brainstorming thought process, we created:

- ✓ 18 rendered views
- ✓ 6 min 3D walkthrough
- ✓ A Drone shoot was conducted to illustrate the project's vast scale.

Also, the first cut of the project was shown to the client in twenty-five days. It usually takes more than six months for a project to complete. Still, we completed the entire project in four months, including all the necessary changes. This execution is probably a record to have achieved in such a short duration. We made the unthinkable a reality. The client was delighted and was very impressed with our services and professionalism.

The relationship with this client grew gradually. Then we were allotted two more projects and another one is under making too.

Case Study: SAES (Soham Architecture & Engineers Services), Nashik

About the company

Founded in 1996 by Vijay Sanap, SOHAM Architectural Engineering Services (SAES) is an architectural engineering firm dedicated to achieving a design that maximises any project's aesthetic and productive aspects. They have worked on many projects, from single-family residences and holiday resorts to retail outlets, fast food restaurants and high-rise group housing. They are one of the leading Architects and Engineering firms in Nashik city.

Challenges

The client had been in the industry for more than two decades. They have worked with many 3D Freelancers and full-time studios in Nashik and nearby major cities like Pune, Aurangabad, Surat and Ahmedabad. Nashik was always a small town till two years back, i.e. till the year 2020. Over these years, the city has started growing exponentially. The digital thrust which India is experiencing also helped, and being just two hours away from Mumbai also gave the needed impetus. After a new Development plan in Nashik, suddenly real estate started booming. During that period, SAES faced many challenges from its Builders and Developer clients for professional 3D rendering work to market their projects. SAES worked on 3-4 projects from Ahmedabad based studios, but service was the major challenge he was facing from them. One fine day Vijay Sanap saw our advertisement on his Instagram account and contacted us. We met him in Nashik, where he briefed us on his massive upcoming theme-based multi-building residential complex project.

It was challenging as expectations were high. Having worked with many in the past, we had to raise our performance bar.

****

SAES worked on 3-4 projects from Ahmedabad-based studios, but service was the major challenge he was facing from them.

****

Solution

My team and his team started working together to match the wavelength first. We had multiple offline and online meetings to understand his taste in work. Eventually, we gave them two qualities of deliverables for approval. He liked one, so our team was clear about what exactly he needed, and a step-by-step process was outlined. We started sharing the different versions with him and his team, first grey renderings, camera angles, and sequences. Work began to progress further quickly. Finally, the colour renderings were shown to them to get the exact look and feel of the project. There were iterations and back-and-forth communication during this entire process since we were working together the first time. This working pattern is typical when you perform it the first time. We must come on the same page before we can effectively crack the code to surpass their expectations.

A few design elements were very tricky, and ready models were unavailable. Having understood the limitations, the team customized the models so that we don't compromise on the quality of the project.

* *

This working pattern is typical when you perform it the first time. We must come on the same page before we can effectively crack the code to surpass their expectations.

* *

Result

Finally, we successfully delivered the projects in a straight seventy-five days period. The client wanted a three and half minute walkthrough. Still, after seeing the project's outcome, he extended the duration to two minutes. That means a total five- and half-minute walkthrough. Such was the impact of our work, and since they were so happy, the client didn't worry about the extra cost as the scope of work extended. Mr Vijay Sanap called me personally to thank my team and me for bringing out the best results. He was expecting premium quality, but he said you guys gave us "Ultra-premium quality", in his own words. Even before completing 100% of the first assignment, he appointed Weaverbird for another couple of projects: Affordable housing and a premium housing complex. That's the most significant achievement for us. Client satisfaction is essential for us since we are creative people. The joy of creating customized work always inspires creative people.

****

Finally, we successfully delivered the projects in a straight seventy-five days period. The client wanted a three and half minute walkthrough. Still, after seeing the project's outcome, he extended the duration to two minutes. That means a total five- and half-minute walkthrough.

****

Case Study: Indu Builders and Developers, Bilaspur-Chattisgarh

About the company

Indu Builders and Developers is part of Indu Group - Bilaspur. They are into multiple businesses like Petrol pumps, Gas agencies etc., other than the Real estate.

It's a family business managed by three brothers. Elder brother Mr Shailesh Agarwal manages the real estate business. Bilaspur is a tier three city in Chhattisgarh, India. Its mission is to move from a typical individual house to make people live in gated community projects. The thought is to improve the lifestyle of simple people.

His dream to make a real estate development project in Mumbai, for which he spent three years in Mumbai, couldn't be successful. He decided to return to Bilaspur and re-live his dream of becoming a builder and developer there.

Challenges

Mr Shailesh Agarwal had a land bank of 400 acres. He was starting his first project on 45 acres near High court, Bilaspur.

He focused on selling plots and building row houses, whichever customers needed. He thought of making extra income from construction also. But he realised very soon that his properties wouldn't be sold without marketing. He thought of making the 3D walkthrough to attract customers and contacted Weaverbird through his project Architect Amit Vadnere.

He asked me to come over to Bilaspur. He sponsored the entire trip. It was another experience as I had to invest my time there, staying for a few days but leaving for Mumbai not before closing the deal.

* *

But he realised very soon that his properties wouldn't be sold without marketing. He thought of making the 3D walkthrough to attract customers and contacted Weaverbird through his project Architect Amit Vadnere.

* *

Solution

The strategy was clear again. We helped him with Drone shoots, and that worked brilliantly for him. We realized he was very selective and had an excellent eye for detail. Landscapes were a significant challenge; we had to capture them effectively as it was the major challenge. Sometimes when the client takes extreme interest can also prove to be a hindrance on a lighter side. Still, we had to change, edit and amend frequently and the team was quite stressed out as selecting the trees and plantations was challenging. We realize this can happen with a few. Such challenges sometimes also help because they get the best out of us, creatively challenging us. It is a good problem to face as client satisfaction matters the most. Then the first wave of the Covid hit the project, and it went on hold for almost six months. Post that period;

he again invited my team to start. It was good to work on this project again.

Result

And then, in the subsequent three months exactly, we delivered the project with a six-minute walkthrough, rendering images and many other 3D services. The client thanked my team for having kept the same intensity and consistency despite the project being exceeded beyond nine months due to Covid. This Covid period was one of the toughest for all as the pandemic affected many businesses besides the health of many. The client appreciated the team never lost control and kept their nerves till project completion without compromising the efforts and quality. Our relationship with the client was firmly established due to the extended execution period. We are already in talks for another fifteen acres as part of the second phase.

We were delighted to know that our work helped his sales, and he experienced rapid growth. Eighty per cent of the project is sold out.

* *

The client thanked my team for having kept the same intensity and consistency despite the project being exceeded beyond nine months due to Covid.

* *

Case Study: JBD - Oakwood by Sri Group, Mumbai

About the company

Sri Group has been in the business of providing quality real estate since 1974.

It has built over ten million square feet to hold ten thousand apartments. The group's repertoire is driven by a simple philosophy that has enabled them to develop properties ranging from residential and commercial estates to townships, entertainment facilities, hotels and health centres. A professional management team has ensured that owning an apartment at Oakwood is a delightful proposition.

Challenges

I know Mr Dhaval Kamdar, Director of Sri Group, because of BNI (the global networking organisation). We both are members of BNI from different chapters. When we came on board, Dhaval was clear about what he needed for his project as far as 3D rendering work was concerned. Still, he was entering the Mumbai Northwest (Nalasopara) market for the first time, so he was unsure about customers' reaction to the Oakwood property. It was a tricky situation to be in. He briefly told my team that 3D renderings' quality must be awe-inspiring. "I want to use 3D renderings as the biggest tool for marketing". After hearing this, we knew we were heading towards another challenging project in hand and will have to perform really well to meet the client's expectations. His project elevations weren't finalised, which was the biggest challenge in showing the client various elevation options. He just had primary elevations done by his Architect.

Solution

I suggested to Dhaval that since this location has a few critical benefits, let's capture this location's advantages through a Drone shoot. I insisted we fly the drone nearby and in and around the project. He agreed to it immediately. I suggested to him India's leading Drone shoot team. With the help of my project manager, we directed the drone team to get relevant shots which were essential for the project. We used these drone shots in our 3D walkthrough in a realistic manner along with the upcoming metro services. My team told him to share the elevation references, which helped them get it right per his requirements.

Result

The client, with multiple rounds of corrections and modifications in elevations, finally got what he needed and was extremely happy and satisfied, which he was expecting from my team and me. We delivered him the walkthrough, rendering still images. This was just the beginning. After seeing our work and experiencing our services, he decided to offload more work to Weaverbird's kitty. He offered us to make 3D virtual tours and real-time walkable walkthroughs with the help of Virtual gear. A few weeks later, these were also delivered successfully. The same client keeps referring us to his Builder friends, and we are also his first choice for new projects soon.

Good work attracts more work. The reward for good work is more work - nothing to complain about.

* *

After seeing our work and experiencing our services, he decided to offload more work to Weaverbird's kitty. He offered us to make 3D virtual tours and real-time walkable walkthroughs with the help of Virtual gear

* *

Case Study: Aparna Group, Hyderabad

About the company

Aparna Enterprises Limited (AEL) is a part of the esteemed Aparna Group. Founded in 1990, AEL prides itself on having the largest market share in South India. AEL is in building-material products like RMC (Ready Mix Concrete), uPVC windows and doors, tiles and sanitaryware fittings. Associated with several landmark projects for over twenty-nine years, AEL is now highly renowned for setting benchmarks in technology, research, design and quality.

Challenges

Aparna Enterprise required twenty High-Definition 3D Renderings to present their broad product portfolio to the prospects and convert them into revenues. But before getting us on board, they were associated with another agency. Because they did not receive their expected photorealistic output, AEL decided to switch. Then, one of the company's members recommended our services, and AEL approached us. AEL is based in Hyderabad; we had a telephonic conversation with them and received the brief over the phone.

* *

Aparna Enterprise required twenty High-Definition 3D Renderings to present their broad product portfolio to the prospects and convert them into revenues.

* *

After identifying and understanding their needs, we pitched them our ideas, and they loved them. After receiving a go-ahead, our 3D experts commenced the work on the aesthetic 3D design options. AEL just had primary elevations done by his Architect as inputs to us.

Solution

Our 3D Visualising team worked closely with the team at AEL. To test the waters, we started sharing reference images with the client. This activity gave us a better understanding of their vision and preferences. With mutual understanding and support, we progressed to creating one render a day and delivered the twenty 3D renders in the stipulated time frame.

Result

We delivered realistic photo renders as per our promise. We only could do this because of the trust and mutual understanding we share with our clients. Client satisfaction is our only endeavour; it has helped us grab another project from the same client.

We are now their full-time 3D Partners!

* * *

Turning Points

"It is strange but true, that the most important turning points of life often come at the most unexpected time and in the most unexpected ways"

Napoleon Hill

If someone had told me when I had passed out of my college that I would start a business of my own, a full-fledged 3D visualizing & animation studio, honestly, I would have laughed. Circumstances changed; I failed, was down, and was stressed, but there was always light at the end of the tunnel. The journey was not easy, and I'm still learning, but I was fortunate to have also met some great people on this path.

The turning points were many, but here are a few on top of my mind:

- The year 2015–2018 It was sluggish growth, and I was not happy with what we were achieving. Usually, the first three years are crucial to surviving and the next two to get the right track, but we were unsure how things would shape up. I witnessed how an ex-colleague senior to me had established, and his growth was worth noticing. It also told me that there's scope, space and hope for me. That motivated me to raise my performance bar.

  What mattered was to research to understand why we were not getting the desired results. What were we lacking? I could see my colleague's efforts, strategies, and hard work motivated me further.

  I discovered he is an MBA and is extremely good in marketing, doing activities that get him potential leads. With his sales techniques, he was able to close the deals successfully.

- I also studied other successful entrepreneurs from the advertising and creative industry. To my surprise, it was the same story with everyone, i.e. one or the other co-founder was good in marketing or networking.

Then I invested in learning and attending pieces of training. After taking personal coaching from Rajiv Talreja and the team, I have started aggressively focusing on marketing. Wherein earlier I focused on leads coming naturally or using contacts from ex-colleagues or college friends, I started getting into concentrated strategies.

****

To my surprise, it was the same story with everyone, i.e. one or the other co-founder was good in marketing or networking.

****

- I devoted fifty percent of my time entirely to marketing activities. I joined networking forums such as BNI and IIID. I started using social media platforms, which became my potent weapon for marketing. I took a few more steps and invested in making vlogs, reels, and posts to generate that interest in what we do.

Initially, I wasn't comfortable and used to be constantly anxious. But then I knew I needed to do this, must move out of my comfort zone to get desired results. I read in the book "Secrets of Millionaire Mind" by T Harv Eker

- Success lies out of comfort zone; if you need to see different results, you need to do things differently.

Read more: https://millionairemindevents.com/secrets-of-the-millionaire-mind/

- Like a typical entrepreneur, initially, I was doing everything by myself. Slowly I got a team on board for creating content and uploading posts on Social media platforms. Things become easier once you have a strong team with you. I focused more on conversion than on generating leads for myself.

  Now it's been three years I have been doing this regularly, and we have been receiving good leads, proper interest, relevant reactions and people have been observing and following us globally.

- Having understood the importance of a good website very early, we invested a lot in creating one and updating it regularly. Nowadays, any prospect checks our social media presence, websites and google reviews before contacting us. I can proudly say that we are doing exceptionally well as far as this activity is concerned. Weaverbird receives forty percent of business from networking forums like BNI and the rest from referrals and marketing leads.

- Way back in the year 2013, I got into cycling. Initially, I used to go cycling with my school friend. Then we became a part of a Cycling community named Mulund Riders - today, I'm a core committee member of the Cycling Club, which has more than 500 riders. We conduct rides, events, and activities to encourage more riders and healthy life.

****

Weaverbird receives forty percent of business from networking forums like BNI and the rest from referrals and marketing leads.

****

So, when I started my firm Weaverbird way back in 2015, I was already into cycling and was very comfortable with fellow riders. Then after a year, I realized I didn't know my fellow riders were professionally doing so well. Some are reputed Doctors and Chartered Accountants, a few are in the big-time manufacturing business, some are in retail outlets, some have successful jewellery brands, and some are in the service industry.

This pool of people motivated me to get into Entrepreneurship which has MY time, family time, vacations and, more importantly, freedom.

This group was crucial to changing my thinking and giving me further insight into the business. If you ask any layman what you need first thing in business, he will say clients and capital. But I learnt from these people that the first thing you need in business is Courage, a good Mindset and Patience. If you have all this, then only enter into business. Rest will follow, and you can build clients, money, and a team. These fundamentals were essential for me to understand.

* *

But I learnt from these people that the first thing you need in business is Courage, a good Mindset and Patience.

* *

Here are a few takeaways from the great people I met at Mulund riders who are my buddies now:

- From Suresh Parmar, I have learned how to manage your contacts and why you should participate in exhibitions and events. Today he is one of the biggest exporters of sesame globally from India.

- From Vinod Tejwani, I have learned how to build your team and a culture in your organization.

- From Kamal Gada, I have learned how to balance life with your basic needs, future expenses, investments, and construct an MY time.

- From Kalpesh Pasad, I have learned how to focus on quality products, channelizing and money recovery.

- Another big turning point was when we started Weaverbird. In the first two years, i.e. 2015-17, we used to do in-house, from modelling to rendering. Whenever we had to do a High resolution in 8k or 10k or even for a 3D walkthrough, there was a challenge. My office systems used to take a lot of time, and the team kept rendering at night till the following day. That means 24 hours my machines, used to be switched on which impacted electricity bills.

If the current sometimes goes off, my team would again have to put on renderings the next day. This process and experience were getting stressful. Our systems were getting occupied, and we could not do any other work.

Till I came to know about render farm from my team members. I came from creative and advertising background and was not aware of this. I didn't know render farm.

Render farm is mainly based in China, where we upload renders, pay money in advance, and get your renders quickly. For example, if my internal systems took 12 hours for any typical 30-second HD walkthrough. In render farms, it takes just 45 mins. In that case, we save a lot of time, eventually benefiting my customers.

- Later I figured out Render farm has been used by many professional full-time studios, even those in the industry for several years. Nothing new to my industry, but we utilize render farm very strategically. We negotiated with render farm regarding guaranteed billing from Weaverbird, for which we asked for better pricing, eventually benefiting my customer.

- We don't do in-house renders, especially for 8k-10k resolutions or walkthroughs. We directly upload on render farms which benefited my company and me for a 2x growth in terms of business.

- The results matter, and clients don't worry about where you get your renders done. They need the jobs at the earliest without compromising on quality and service.

  That's precisely what we do. As one of our strong value propositions, we bet or grab new projects on the fastest delivery point.

* * *

Some Great Books I Have Read

"Good books don't give up all their secrets at once"

Stephen King

Reading is a part of my life–constant reading and updating matter the most. There's so much to learn. A few books I've read have had a lasting impact on me, and I often refer to them. Every time I get hold of them and flip through some pages, I learn something new. Books inspire; they are your best friends as you are never alone with a good book in your hand.

Here are a few great books I've read:

1. Secrets of the Millionaire Mind - by T Harv Eker

How to find out Money Blueprint.

How to manage your money game in 5 various forms/buckets

- money for expenses
- money for travel
- money for play/fun
- money for investments
- money for donation

Secrets of the Millionaire Mind reveals the missing link between wanting success and achieving it! Have you ever wondered why some people seem to get rich easily, while others are destined for a life of financial struggle? Is the difference found in their education, intelligence, skills, timing, work habits, contacts, luck, or their choice of jobs, businesses, or investments? The shocking answer is: None of the above! In his ground-breaking Secrets of the Millionaire Mind, T. Harv Eker states: "Give me five minutes, and I can predict your financial future for the rest of your life!" Eker does this by identifying your "money and success blueprint." We all have a personal money blueprint ingrained in our subconscious minds, and it is this blueprint, more than anything, that will determine our financial lives. You can know everything about marketing, sales, negotiations, stocks, real estate, and the world of finance, but if your money blueprint is not set for a high level of success, you will never have a lot of money—and if somehow you do, you will most likely lose it! The good news is that now you can actually reset your money blueprint to create natural and automatic success.

Source:https://www.amazon.com/Secrets-Millionaire MindMastering-Wealth/dp/0060763280

This book helped me to change my thinking towards money.

2. Rich Dad Poor Dad - by Robert Kiyosaki

- How to Invest, why to Invest and how to create wealth.

It has since become the #1 Personal Finance book of all time... translated into dozens of languages and sold around the world.

Rich Dad Poor Dad is Robert's story of growing up with two dads – his real father and the father of his best friend, his rich dad – and the ways in which both men shaped his thoughts about money and investing. The book explodes the myth that you need to earn a high income to be rich and explains the difference between working for money and having your money work for you.

Rich Dad Poor Dad...

- Explodes the myth that you need to earn a high income to become rich
- Challenges the belief that your house is an asset
- Shows parents why they can't rely on the school system to teach their kids about money
- Defines once and for all an asset and a liability
- Teaches you what to teach your kids about money for their future financial success.

In many ways, the messages of Rich Dad Poor Dad, messages that were criticized and challenged two decades ago, are more meaningful, relevant and important today than they were 20 years ago.

Source: https://www.richdad.com/ , https://www.amazon.

com/Rich-Dad-Poor-Teach-Middle/dp/1612680194

A book everyone should read. While the concepts of money and earning have been taught to us by our parents, we all need a "Rich Dad" to think differently.

3. The 5am Club - by Robin Sharma

- Why morning practise is so important

- Your morning sets your entire day

- Balancing 4 important Empires - Phychology, Emotions, Spirtuality and Physciality

Part manifesto for mastery, part playbook for genius-grade productivity and part companion for a life lived beautifully, the 5 am club is a work that will transform your life. Forever. Legendary leadership and elite performance expert Robin Sharma introduced The 5 AM Club concept over twenty years ago, based on a revolutionary morning routine that has helped his clients maximize their productivity, activate their best health and bulletproof their serenity in this age of overwhelming complexity. Now, in this life-changing book, handcrafted by the author over a rigorous four-year period, you will discover the early-rising habit that has helped so many accomplish epic results while upgrading their happiness, helpfulness and feelings of aliveness. Through an enchanting and often amusing story about two struggling strangers who meet an eccentric tycoon who becomes their secret mentor, The 5 AM Club will walk you through. How great geniuses, business titans and the world's wisest people start their mornings to produce astonishing achievements? A little-known formula you can use instantly to wake up early feeling inspired, focused and flooded with a fiery drive to get the most out of each day. A step-by-step method to protect the quietest hours of daybreak so you have time for exercise, self-renewal and personal growth. A neuroscience-based practice proven to help make it easy to rise while most people are sleeping, giving you precious time for yourself to think, express your creativity and begin the day peacefully instead of being rushed. Insider-only tactics to defend your gifts, talents and dreams against digital distraction and trivial diversions so you enjoy fortune, influence and a magnificent impact on the world.

Source: https://www.robinsharma.com/book/the-5am-club, https://www.amazon.in/AM-Club-Your-Morning-Elevate/dp/9387944891

An absolute eye-opener for anyone. Robin Sharma's series of books are a treat but this clearly stands out.

4. Brave New Work – by Aaron Dignan

How to manage your operations. These things are very important in successful organisations. Structure, Strategy, Meetings, Workflow, Information, Resources, Authority and Purpose

What's stopping you from doing the best work of your life?

The way we work is broken. It takes forever to get anything done. Meetings and emails are incessant. Bureaucracy stifles talent and creativity. Is this really the best we can do?

Aaron Dignan teaches companies how to eliminate red tape, tap into collective intelligence, and rethink long-held traditions that no longer make sense. In Brave New Work, he shows you how to revolutionize the way you, your team and your company works forever. He says:

- Have fewer but better meetings
- Create a culture of honesty, transparency and trust

- Cut down on rules to be more efficient
- Be more agile and adaptive
- Reignite passion and energy throughout your organisation

Source: https://www.bravenewwork.com/ , https://www.amazon.in/Brave-New-Work-Reinvent-Organization/dp/0525536205

An excellent book which helped me shape up my business.

5. What got you here you won't get you there - by Marshal Goldsmith

-How successful become more successful by following right practices, right habits

This book is a much-needed reality check for those high up on the corporate ladder. If you already are a successful leader, such a paradigm shift may be precisely what you need.

Here are 3 lessons that can help top leaders see through the blind spots in their perception:

1. People often succeed despite their flaws - but believe

that they did because of them.

2. Avoiding mistakes should be celebrated as an important part of growth.

3. At the top, it is all about helping others shine.

If you are ready to open your eyes to what's holding you back – this book is just right for you.

Source:https://www.amazon.in/What-Got-Here-Wont-There/dp/0739342231 ; https://marshallgoldsmith.com/book-page-what-got-you-here/

6. Lead or Bleed – by Rajiv Talreja

Entrepreneurs and Corporate Leaders often find themselves in a fire fighting mode because their Next Line Leadership team either lack competence, confidence, commitment and/or ownership.

These Entrepreneurs and Corporate Leaders often find themselves under stress and end up creating a limiting belief about what's possible to be achieved as a team.

Goals set are either safe or are often missed, stakeholders are left unhappy, stress levels are high or the team is complacent and team members are disengaged. In such an environment, leadership is just a jargon used for describing something abstract and unreal.

Entrepreneurs and Corporate Leaders need a proven system of engaging with their teams:

- To develop competence of team members on-the Job.
- Set & achieve goals that are challenging, inspiring and engaging.
- Solve the REAL problems at the root cause level rather than the symptoms level.
- Manage performance on a daily, weekly, monthly and quarterly basis to stay on track and achieve break through goals.

LEARN HOW...

- Learn a Proven System of Leadership which can allow you to balance between Strategic Growth, Operational Excellence and People Development.

- Learn how to engage people to build a High Performance Team.
- Learn what have been the Success Mantras of Inspiring CEOs and Entrepreneurs.
- Learn the Leadership Philosophies of India's 50 Great Workplaces.

Source:https://www.amazon.in/LEAD-BLEED-Entrepreneurs-ACCELERATIONG-PERFORMANCE-ebook/dp/B01DSVYWQK , https://rajivtalreja.com/product/lead-or-bleed/

My personal coaching with Rajiv Talreja was the biggest turning point of my life. He helped me to think differently, shape up the business and build an enterprise.

* * *

My Principles And The People I Follow

"Success is more permanent when you achieve it without destroying your principles"

Walter Cronkite

Principle is fundamental truth or proposition that serves as the foundation for a system of belief or behaviour or for a chain of reasoning.

I always used to think, why do we say "he or she is a person of principles".

What is it that attracts us to a person's behaviour or thinking?

The answer was the principles they followed. This practice is not easy, mind you. It has to be very tough to stick to your principles. There are temptations, diversions, and people who can influence easy paths to take, but the ones who can handle these will go a long way. The ten principles I follow & practice:

1. Courage:

It means mental or moral strength to venture, persevere, and withstand danger, fear, or difficulty.

Coming from a lower-middle-class family, I had to show courage. It wasn't easy. As mentioned, my family always doubted my ability but eventually supported me and saw that spark. From cycling and public speaking to finally even writing this book needed courage.

Being courageous helped me venture into unknown or inexperienced territories. In the earlier days, it was more enthusiasm. Still, the results were more effective when I started taking calculated and informed risks.

2. Mindset:

As you enter each moment, your brain triggers a mindset that offers a thought, belief, feeling, or attitude. This mindset influences how you will engage at the moment presented. In other words, your behaviour is directly affected by the perspective you adopt each moment.

A mindset of a winner is essential, and thanks to my friends at the cycling club, this quality seeped in. A positive and right attitude proved to be the foundation of my success.

3. Patience:

It is the capacity to accept or tolerate delay, problems, or suffering without annoyance or anxiety.

Oh! I needed a lot of this, and fortunately, I did not wilt under pressure, lack of results or support. I had to fight it out with a lot of patience. In entrepreneurship, not reacting to situations of intense anger, frustration or results is crucial.

4. Gratitude:

It is the quality of being thankful and being ready to show appreciation for and return kindness.

A quality which got imbibed because of the people I operate with. BNI taught us more to give than expect. But this principle of expressing gratitude generates more and more gains for us. It generally gives you a feeling of satisfaction.

5. Honest with myself:

Knowing our limitations, not getting too ambitious and being ruthlessly honest in our dealings have benefited me in leaps and bounds. It is a tough path, but to a great extent, my humble background, upbringing and the people I spend my time with influenced me.

6. Accept failures:

There are times when the chips are down. Over these years, I've understood not all business is for me; everything cannot work in our favour. The more I absorbed this and took it in my stride, the less stressed I got.

7. Success:

Success is the accomplishment of an aim or purpose. I needed to set goals, set specific performance benchmarks, and aim at something rather than being happy with what was happening. After the initial struggle, my confidence grew when people started appreciating my work and placing repeat orders. We started celebrating success then.

With success, one needs to get humble and calm also.

As a team, we celebrate success but equally celebrate new initiatives.

8. Delegation:

Delegation is assigning authority to another person to carry out specific activities. It is the process of distributing and entrusting work to another person and, therefore, one of the core concepts of management leadership. This principle helped me graduate and mature. From an "I, Me, Myself" for everything, it is now our team, our people and a collective & engaging way of doing business.

9. Freedom:

This freedom has only to do with creative freedom. Entering entrepreneurship helped me live my life. It helped me do what I wanted to without compromising my personal life.

The freedom to take on business calls, try new things, and challenge me helped me raise the performance bar further.

Entrepreneurship also gets you power, but it is crucial to utilize this power constructively.

10. Consistency:

Someone consistent always behaves in the same way, has the same attitudes towards people or things around them, or achieves the same level of consistent success in their endeavours. The foundation is about the processes, systems, long-term approach, a helping nature, consultative behaviour and putting the other person's benefit more in mind than his.

One needs to celebrate success, but that's for a short period. As mentioned earlier, we give more importance to new initiatives - celebrated more- giving consistent drive to excel further.

The People - My inspiration & why -

Ratan Tata - one of my biggest inspiration. His corporate success is known to all, but he inspires me more for his patriotic personality. I truly resonate with him. One of the biggest Corporate houses, The Tata Group, the way they structure their business, keep re-inventing themselves, and the sheer employment they have generated for Indians and people abroad truly motivates me.

I will be delighted to grow the Indian economy and help

people by creating more jobs in my organisation.

There are so many things we can learn from this great man. Here are some core values of The Tata Group:
Core values:

Tata has always been a values-driven organisation. These values continue to direct the growth and business of Tata companies.

The five core Tata values underpinning the way we do business are:

Integrity

We will be fair, honest, transparent and ethical in our conduct; everything we do must stand the test of public scrutiny.

Responsibility

We will integrate environmental and social principles in our businesses, ensuring that what comes from the people goes back to the people many times over.

Excellence

We will be passionate about achieving the highest standards of quality, always promoting meritocracy.

Pioneering

We will be bold and agile, courageously taking on challenges, using deep customer insight to develop innovative solutions.

Unity

We will invest in our people and partners, enable continuous learning, and build caring and collaborative relationships based on trust and mutual respect.

Every time I read these core values, I get further inspired.

Source: https://www.tata.com/about-us/tata-values-purpose

Mukesh Ambani - I have been reading about his growth journey in the last fifteen years. Though Dhirubhai, his father, had already created a legacy, he has transformed Reliance in a colossal manner. The planning with which he enters any business changes the rules of the game, which is inspiring.

He always hires the best of talent, and post entering the B2C markets, the way he has emphasized on the branding side also is so impressive.

Wealth creation is a lesson learned from him. His ability to think far ahead, invest in tomorrow's technologies and build a big canvas is a true inspiration.

Narendra Modi – Nothing to do with the political side, but his ability to not react aggressively, and being so calm and organised is a treat to observe. I always see him as a great marketer with his superb communication skills. With a complex country like India comprising various religions and people of multiple backgrounds, it takes something to connect with everyone, and he has mastered this quality.

AB de Villiers – A 360 degrees player. A very calm and calculative personality which helps him get great results consistently. Never have I seen him getting wild on the cricket field. His attitude speaks volumes of his character, something every entrepreneur can take a cue from.

Gaur Gopal Das – I follow him blindly. Whatever he says connects to me as he talks about reality and practicality. He says, whatever you need in life, you have to first focus on that thing. To change a life, instead, change yourself. I have been following a few of his best practices daily, which also impacts me professionally.

* * *

Looking Ahead

"The best way to create the future is to create it"

Peter Drucker

The future looks exciting. Weaverbird is on its way to strengthening, consolidating and reaching higher scales.

From a turnover of close to a crore in the FY 2021-22, our visionary goal is to reach (a term taught by my coach Rajiv Talreja) Rs. 2 crores.

How would we do this?

- Reach out more to the tier two and tier three cities in India. While the metros are blossoming, a vastly untapped market is waiting to be catered to. I will not say there is no competition, but there's scope to make a mark. The blue ocean strategy works here. Why concentrate fully on red oceans where there is intense competition? There is enormous scope to get value more out of these tier two and three cities. The business there is consistent, manageable and profitable also.

****

The blue ocean strategy works here. Why concentrate fully on red oceans where there is intense competition? There is enormous scope to get value more out of these tier two and three cities.

****

- Digitization has enabled us to spread more effectively, saving tremendous time, money and energy. We will continue to strengthen our tech side by investing wisely. After people, my priority is to show an edge using the technology which a few can bring to the table.

- We already are working in the global markets. Still, the UK will be the next destination to establish a firm footing. Next on the radar is Canada, where already we are penetrating. From the right team selection, learning their language and working patterns, and adapting global practices, we are committed to spreading our business beyond the Indian shores.

- Growing business strategically with associates and partners is also a top priority. We do not see ourselves becoming a five-hundred-employee company but definitely want to indirectly see a thousand people being associated with us. After forming the core group more deeply with the best of talent on board, we will grow through a vast network, almost along the lines of a franchise or partnering model. The term asset-light is a fantastic term I learned. IT companies worldwide are nimble, asset-light and budgeted to grow strategically, and we are also a technology company.

- We intend to become a private limited company by the Q2 of the FY 2022-23. This entity transformation is going to be a significant milestone for us. A dream come true. It may sound like nothing important for many, but we have been working with a definite purpose to achieve this.

- We intend to get a strategic investor on Board with the above development. We are already in talks with a technology firm who should come on Board soon. Most importantly, they will get value to the company with their network, engagement and focus on growing the business. A time comes in every business when it matures. It needs that impetus to get a further push, a drive, ideas and strategic directions to fuel growth. Our time has come.

- Building the Weaverbird brand further is another top priority I have been working on for some time. My idea is to additionally give the required push and establish a substantial recall value. Today, like how everyone knows the names of L&T, Reliance, and P&G, whether related or not related to them in any form, I want Weaverbird to be recognized as the number one brand in the 3D industry.

- The biggest asset of my firm is the people who work for me and the ones who will come on board ahead. Offering ESOPs - Employee Stock Ownership Plan is my top priority for the team to enjoy the fruits of labour and profits. I also see a strong Board being formed for good governance, business strategy and growth monitoring.

****

- The late 90s up to the year 2000 belonged to the internet explosion. Then came the Android revolution, and mobile phones changed everything. We saw the stories of Blackberry and Nokia and how they once ruled the segments to falling off completely. Then came the Apple era and the advent of a massive tech boom. Digitization became the buzzword globally, and India was not far back. In the last three years post-Covid, India's thrust has further exploded.

  We now hear AI, VR, Blockchain and 3D being the industries to watch.

  The 3D industry will explode, and the need for these services is already being felt in all sectors.

  Why am I so bullish in this industry? Here's an overview of the industry:

- The global visualization and 3D rendering market reached a value of nearly USD 2.2 billion in 2021. As we advance, the market is projected to grow at a CAGR of 22.1% during the forecast period of 2022-27. It is expected to reach a value of USD 7.3 billion by 2027.

New Products/Services we can focus:

1. Metaverse

A network of 3D virtual worlds focused on social connection, and it can be defined as a simulated digital environment that uses AR and VR. With the help of Blockchain technology, along with concepts from digital media.

2. NFT (Non-fungible token)

It's generally built using the same programming as cryptocurrency, like Bitcoin or Ethereum, but that's where the similarity ends. Physical money and cryptocurrencies are "fungible," meaning they can be traded or exchanged for one another.

3. Proptech (Property Technology)

Proptech, also known as real estate technology, applies information technology and platform economics to real estate markets. It reduces paperwork and makes transactions quicker, more efficient, and more secure. Customers can also check property through VR.

9 Industries That Cannot Do without 3D Modelling

(adapted from https://www.cadcrowd.com/blog/3d-modelling-uses-9-industries-that-cannot-do-without-it/)

Let us look at nine specific industries that use this technique frequently. 3D modelling has revolutionized these industries and helped indefinitely improve their processes and products.

This list is not exhaustive, but it features the most notable examples:

1. Engineering

Engineering has developed beyond our wildest dreams. We now have an array of complex machinery for many different industries. Precision engineering, for example, may require the use of high-powered laser cutters that can produce sheet metal specs down to the smallest measurements. How do you think these machines are designed?

3D modelling allows visualizing their machinery and processes in greater detail. A machine with hundreds of small parts can look at each 3D part independently. In addition, they can also use 3D modelling to join the pieces together to form the whole machine. This ensures that everything fits and works as it should. It reduces errors and also reduces waste and needless expenditure.

We no longer need to use pen and paper blueprints for engineering processes. 3D modelling can be used instead in a fraction of the time and cost. 3D modelling has brought engineering into the modern world and helped replace many outdated techniques that were no longer efficient.

2. Manufacturing

Manufacturing is continually evolving. In ages past, products were made by hand using slow and painstaking techniques. As time moved on, we started seeing automation being introduced.

Initially, 3D printing was mainly considered a novelty. The printers were expensive, and people would use them to create items of no use.

However, as the technology became more accessible, it started to see greater use. Now, 3D printing is used for a myriad of different purposes.

We can create anything from tools and office equipment to whole buildings. "Rapid prototyping" is quick. You will hear the term Rapid prototyping very often in times to come.

Furthermore, it creates little waste and allows for excellent creativity.

3D printing is based on 3D modelling. Manufacturers will first create 3D models on a computer. This design will then be sent to the 3D printer, and the final product will be made. 3D modelling should hopefully revolutionize the manufacturing industry for years to come.

3. Architecture

For decades, architectural design services have used traditional methods to visualize structures. The tried and tested process used a combination of blueprints and 2D technical drawings. These drawings would show various plans and elevations of a structure using scale measurements. You may have a handful of different drawings just for one room of a structure - that's not even considering things such as foundation drawings and reinforcements.

3D modelling has changed all of this. Traditional architectural methods are becoming a thing of the past. It is no longer efficient or productive to use old-fashioned methods when 3D modelling can provide so much more in a fraction of the time. Architects can now create complete structures using 3D modelling programs. There is no need for heaps of drawings and materials - simply one 3D modelling file showcases every building aspect.

Not only is this fantastic for visualization purposes, but it also gives greater creativity and flexibility. Suppose an element of the building doesn't work or is undesirable. In that case, it can just be changed in the 3D modelling program with no adverse consequences. Moreover, as you are creating 3D graphics, you can essentially create what you can imagine - this opens the door for new and exciting types of architectural design.

4. Filmmaking

Look at filmmaking 30 years ago and compare it to today's world. In ages past, CGI (Computer Generated Imagery) was unheard of - we had to use stop motion and other techniques. Since the 80s, CGI has become hugely influential in films.

3D modelling is an integral part of the modern filmmaking process.

Film producers can use 3D modelling to create fantastic CGI graphics that are impossible through physical production processes. Moreover, we can realize entire 3D modelling worlds and new planets - the possibilities are literally endless.

Think of some of the recent films that have been released - take the Marvel superhero series, for example, with films such as Avengers: Infinity War. How many of those films would be possible without 3D modelling and CGI? Practically none of them! Would they have been able to create characters such as Groot or Iron Man? Would they have been able to realize worlds and regions such as Wakanda and Titan? Probably not.

Due to 3D modelling, adventurous film projects can be realized, and we can enjoy the cinema like never before. Film projects that were previously a dream are now possible through CGI and 3D modelling.

5. Video Game Design

Think back to the dawn of video games - we had excellent

2D pixelated graphics with such treasured games as Space Invaders and Pong. Look now at the type of video games we have. 3D modelling technology has played an enormous role in advancing video game graphics.

Developers can create 3D items in astounding detail. Games can show vast open worlds. They can also show human faces and animals in incredibly lifelike detail. Developers can even recreate the sea, water droplets, and waves. In addition to this, they can create other lifelike particles such as dust, smoke, and weather conditions.

If we look at some of the recent games that have been released, we can see just how important 3D modelling is to this industry. We have God of War for the PS4, for example, which throws the player into Norse Mythology where you can confront gods and monsters.

On the other hand, we have games such as Grand Theft Auto that allow you to freely explore huge cityscapes. Don't forget the amazing sports games that use 3D modelling and face capture techniques to recreate the features of stars such as Ronaldo and Kevin Durant.

6. Healthcare

As with many other industries in this list, 3D modelling has helped improve healthcare and medical science significantly. This process is being used in the pharmaceutical industry in a variety of different ways, some of which we have listed below.

Firstly, 3D modelling can be used to visualize the human body. In the past, medical students looked at such things as plastic skeletons and model organs. Now, we can use modelling to create CGI versions of our bodies. We can look at anything from our circulatory system to the neurons in our brain and the structure of our lungs. This has helped improve our understanding of the human body and teaching techniques.

Secondly, 3D modelling can also be used to help create artificial organs and medical equipment. Researchers can use modelling programs to develop new equipment designs - scalpels and forceps, for example. Furthermore, they can use them with 3D printers or CAD machines to create prototypes for testing.

In short, we now have access to many tools, equipment, and study aids that were not available in years past.

7. Scientific Research

Scientific research and development have exploded in the last 20 decades - this is partly due to 3D modelling. This process has a myriad of different uses in an array of scientific disciplines.

First, we have climate models and projections. 3D modelling has helped transform the way we analyse and predict the weather. Climatologists can use advanced modelling software to create weather zones and simulations. This can help show weather patterns and predict how dangerous natural occurrences such as hurricanes and earthquakes will act and the impact they could have.

Secondly, we have geology and the natural world. Scientists have begun using scanning technology and 3D modelling to map our planet. For example, in some countries, there are extensive cave networks - 3D modelling can be used to map out these caves to explore them.

Finally, chemists can use 3D modelling to look at complex chemical structures of different elements and atoms. They can use it to display practically anything - things that may not be visible by the naked eye, for example.

8. Marketing

Marketing permeates our everyday lives. How often do you see or hear marketing at home, work, or walking down the street? Billboards, TV adverts, flyers, social media - marketing is hugely important in business. Without marketing, companies would be unable to effectively promote their products and raise awareness of their offerings.

Traditionally, photography would have been a primary method of production for marketing pieces. Businesses would hire a professional photographer and undertake a whole studio shoot involving complicated lighting, flashes, and other equipment.

The photographer would take a series of exceptional snaps of the company's products - these would then be used in promotional material. This method was time-consuming and expensive.

Programs such as Photoshop have allowed companies to reduce the need for photography. Combine this with 3D modelling, and businesses can now create marketing materials in a fraction of the time and cost. 3D modelling is fantastic for product catalogues and advertising media.

Products can be placed seamlessly within any environment. Furthermore, textures, patterns, shapes, and sizes can be changed with a few clicks of a mouse. There is less need for props and expensive marketing setups.

9. Industrial Design

Freelance industrial design involves creating machinery, factory layouts, and production processes. 3D modelling has brought unprecedented detail and efficiency to this process. Traditionally, this type of process would be completed using pen and paper and blueprints. Obviously, this is time-consuming. Furthermore, this method is open to human error and misinterpretation.

By using 3D modelling, companies can realise whole facility layouts instantly. Let's look at a food packaging company, for example. They could use 3D modelling to design the floor space of their factory. This could include packaging machines, assembly lines, loading bays, and goods inward. The whole process can be designed down to minute details.

This can significantly improve efficiency. Furthermore, potential bottlenecks in production can be spotted and addressed by visualising the entire factory. 3D modelling is essential for industrial design as it can help create productive and profitable facilities.

Many industries directly couldn't operate efficiently without using 3D modelling and programs such as AutoCAD and SolidWorks. Moreover, 3D modelling opens up new possibilities and drives forward innovation and creativity. As technology improves, we should only see 3D modelling become more accessible and used in a broader range of situations in the future.

Global Market Overview:

https://www.mordorintelligence.com/industry-reports/3d-mapping-and-3d-modelling

- Increasing adoption of 3D technology across multiple industry verticals for catering to the growing demand for emerging applications, ranging from shape analysis, 3D mapping, and 3D modelling, among others, has given rise to the development of 3D mapping and 3D modelling software that can gauge shapes in real-time.

- The 3D-enabling devices, such as cameras, sensors, scanners, global position system (GPS) satellite components, and other 3D content acquisition, create colossal potential across the market.

- Moreover, with significant investments for 3D map applications to be integrated with smartphones, market players, such as Samsung, Nokia, and other OEMs, are entering this market. Online web service providers, such as Amazon Inc. and Microsoft Corp., have also started offering 3D maps on their platforms. For instance, Parrot, a prominent player catering to wireless devices for mobile phones, has positioned its consumer drones for 3D modelling, mapping, and agricultural uses.

- Amid the ongoing outbreak of COVID-19 across the world, the healthcare sector is increasingly adopting robots that use 3D mapping and modelling technology. For instance, The Milagrow Humanoid ELF, an India-based robotics company, mentioned testing Ai-powered robots iMap9 and Humanoid ELF in the COVID-19 ward of AIIMS. The iMap9 is a floor disinfecting robot that can navigate and sanitize the floors without human intervention. It used 3D mapping technology for floor cleaning.

UK 3D Rendering Market Size, by Software, 2015-2026 (USD mn Source: www.gminsights.com

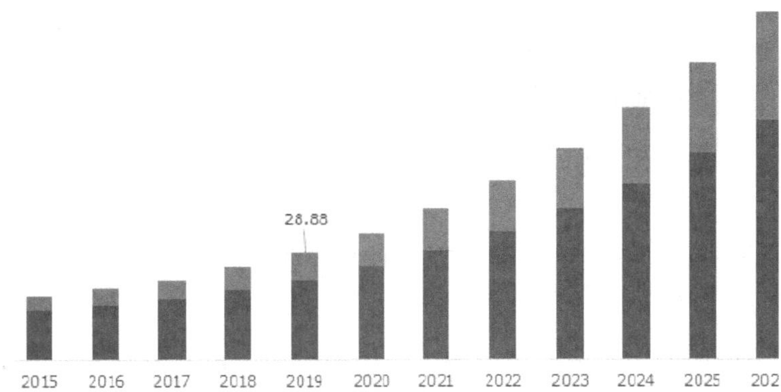

China 3D Rendering Market Size, by Application, 2019-2026 (USD mn)

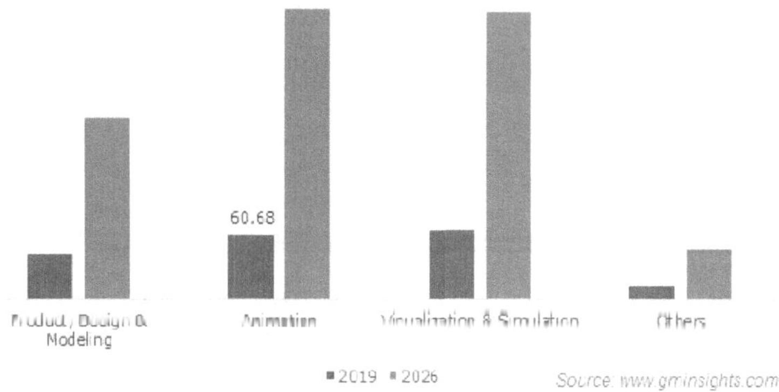

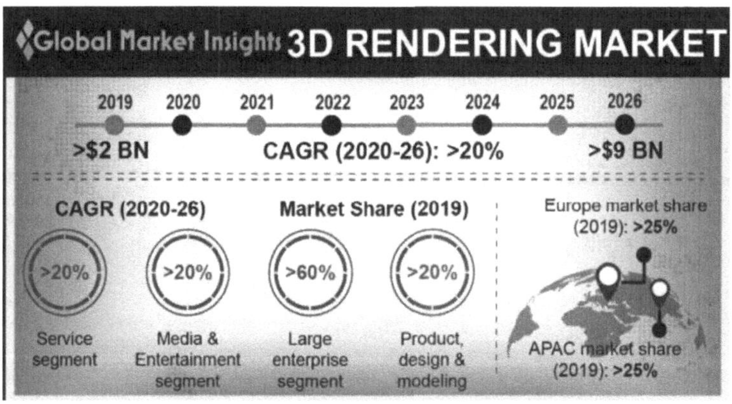

https://www.gminsights.com/industry-analysis/3d-rendering market

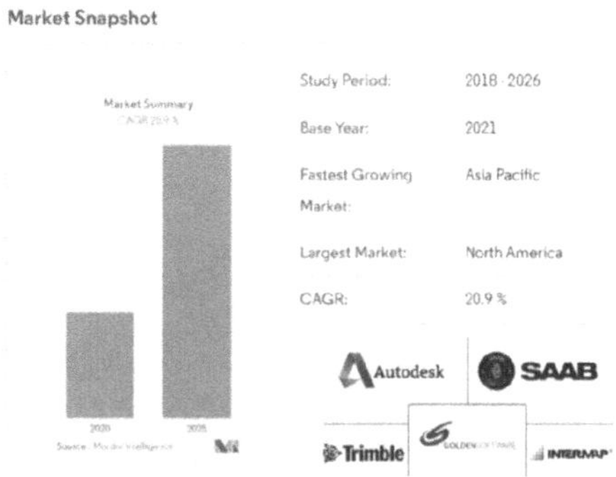

https://www.mordorintelligence.com/industry-reports/3d-mapping-and-3d-modelling

Global Visualisation & 3D Rendering Market Market size by end use (%)Source: www.expertmarketresearch.com

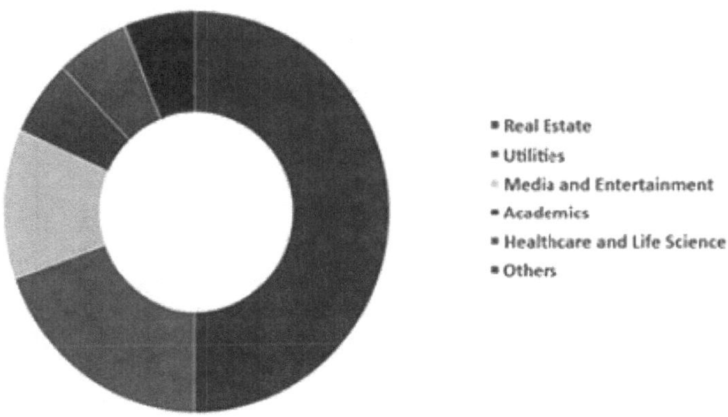

3D Mapping & 3D Modelling Market - growth rate by geography (2020-2025)

US Visualisation & 3D Rendering software market by size and application (2014-2025):

https://www.grandviewresearch.com/industry-analysis/visualization-3d-rendering-software-market

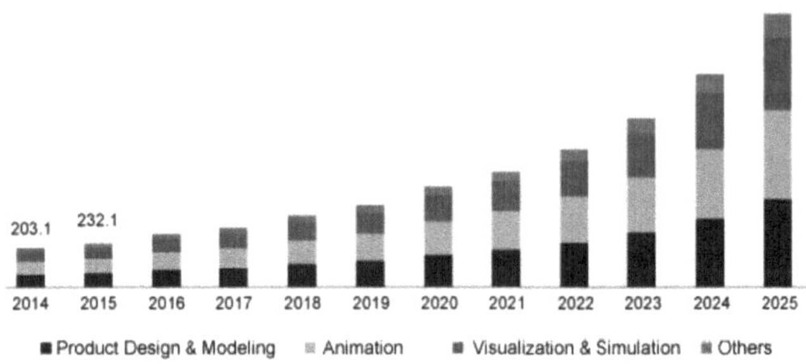

Global visualisation & 3D Rendering software market by region, 2014-24 (in Bn USD):

https://www.ameriresearch.com/visualization-3d-rendering-software-market/

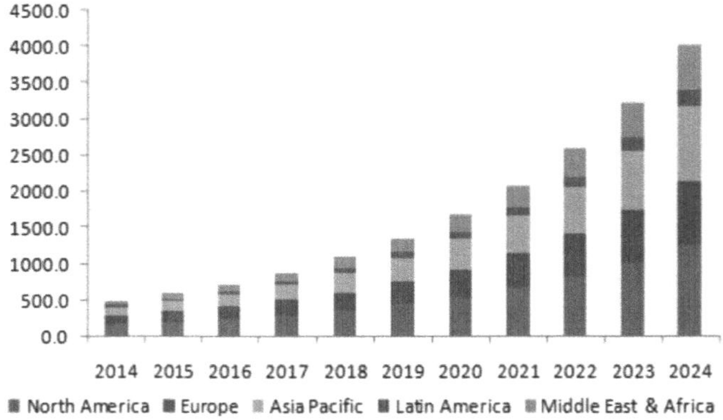

Key Market Trends

Source:https://www.mordorintelligence.com/industry-reports/3d-mapping-and-3d-modelling

Building and Construction to Witness Significant Growth

- Due to fast-paced infrastructural development in various developing regions worldwide, there seems to be a constant up-gradation regarding building designs and architectural requirements.
- Moreover, the architectural industry has been growing considerably. Except for the current temporary setback

in the context of the COVID pandemic, an increasing number of new architectural firms are entering the market with innovative designs and software. They are providing better services such as enhancement in urban planning which is expected to increase the demand for upgraded design technology involving 3D models, and high-end designing software.

- 3D mapping helps in geolocation and making building models of construction sites, buildings, and structures that allow architects to design, plan, and manage site logistics. For instance, Zmapping, a London-based company, provides 3D models to create some of the most detailed and accurate context 3D city models for architects, local authorities, and master planners.

- Rapid urbanization results in increased infrastructure development, thereby increasing the demand for 3D technologies. The development of smart cities in India and China is expected to boost the need for 3D mapping and modelling software.

North America to Hold Significant Share

- Various vendors in the autonomous driving market are gaining investments, which is expected to drive the demand for these solutions. For Instance, Nuro, a company based in Mountain View, California, announced that it had raised USD 940 million in financing from the SoftBank Vision Fund. The company announced that it would use the new financing to expand its delivery service to new geographies, for the addition of new partners, scale its fleet, extend and mature its self-driving technology, and significantly grow its team.

- The US media and entertainment industry is considered to have a significant share worldwide. The rising number of 3D movies and animated movies, which are one of the primary users of this technology and the rising adoption of 3D gaming across the region, are continuously increasing the demand for the 3D mapping and 3D modelling market.

- According to a recent survey of construction stakeholders in the United States, conducted by the International Trade Administration, United States, it is estimated that the country has witnessed a 14% gain in the number of companies willing to build 60% of their projects as green projects by the end of 2018. This is expected to create a massive scope for the market.

* * *

A quick snapshot:

Weaverbird

We specialize in 3D renderings, i.e., virtual reality and motion graphic animation. We offer a variety of services across three distinct verticals. In terms of 3D visualization, we provide 3D walkthroughs, 3D Images, 3D Isometrics, 3D Printing and 3D/2D Plans. In the Animation category, you'll find Audio-Visual Videos, CGI/VFX/Graphics, Explanatory Videos, Corporate Videos, Infographic Videos & Motion graphics. We also offer virtual tours, virtual 3D tours and 360-degree panoramas.

www.facebook.com/weaverbirdcreativesolutions

www.linkedin.com/company/weaverbird-3d-visualization-and-animation-studio/

www.instagram.com/3dweaverbird/

www.youtube.com/channel/UC_yhjyucKFVIJw_64npQIeQ

www.instagram.com/vinodpatilofficial/

www.linkedin.com/in/vinod-patil-3dvisualizationbusinessexpert/

email id: info@weaverbird.co.in

www.weaverbird.co.in

* * *